MULTINATIONAL FINANCIAL MANAGEMENT

INTERNATIONAL FINANCIAL ANALYSIS AND TREASURY MANAGEMENT FOR THE MULTINATIONAL CORPORATION

Surendra K. Kaushik, Ph.D.
Professor of Finance,
Director, Institute of International Banking
Lubin Graduate School of Business
Pace University

Lawrence M. Krackov, M.B.A., J.D.
Vice President and Treasurer,
CBS Records Inc.

New York Institute of Finance

Library of Congress Cataloging-in-Publication Data

Kaushik, S. K., 1944-
Multinational financial management : international financial analysis and treasury management for the multinational corporation Surendra K. Kaushik, Lawrence M. Krackov.
p. cm.
Includes bibliographies and index.
ISBN 0-13-605123-5
1. International business enterprises--Finance--Management.
2. International business enterprises--United States--Finance--Management. I. Krackov, Lawrence M. II. Title.
HG4027.5.K38 1989
658.15'99--dc20 89-32649
CIP

Printed in the United States of America
10 9 8 7 6 5 4 3 2 1

New York Institute of Finance
(NYIF Corp.)
70 Pine Street
New York, NY 10270-0003

Dedicated to our beloved mothers,
Ratni Kaushik and Betty Ruth Krackov,
who provided the initial inspiration
for such endeavors.

Contents

Preface

Corporate financial management concentrates on the various types of financing and resource-allocation decisions that face a corporation's chief financial officer. Since financial decisions affect the company's financial statements as well as its cash flow and valuation, the accounting implications of each strategy must receive equal attention in this decision-making process.

Therefore, this book is aimed at serving the international treasury practitioner as well as the investment analyst or student in making such allocation decisions in a practical and comprehensive manner. It is not an economic treatise, nor is it a speculator's handbook. Instead, this book applies the basic principles of finance and accounting to the international problems and opportunities facing multinational corporations, using U.S. companies as examples.

Four major areas are covered:

1. "International Environment for Financial Decisions" (Part I)
2. "Utilization of International Markets to Support Domestic Operations" (Part II)
3. "Funding and Management of Cash and Capital for Foreign Operations" (Part III)
4. "Protection of Capital of Foreign Corporations" (Part IV)

The international economic and financial systems and markets are covered in the first section. From the multinational corporation's perspective, they represent the environment in which strategic decisions are made and the mechanics of implementation operate. The multinational financial manager's goal is to utilize the economic and financial systems and markets for the strategies and mechanics of implementation discussed in Parts II through IV. Thus, following the first section, information on the systems and markets is again cross-referenced from Parts II through IV because it is required to fully understand the strategies discussed in the next three sections.

The second section is aimed at utilizing the international markets for raw materials, intermediate goods, finished goods, and capital funds to help supply and finance corporate requirements in the United States and to help expand the foreign revenue base through export operations. Many raw materials, intermediate goods, and finished goods used by U.S. corporations for domestic and export businesses can obviously be supplied by other countries. These are often the only source or the best source; or they can offer higher quality, lower prices, or other favorable delivery. Also, at various points in time, both terms and rates in foreign capital markets can be very favorable compared with those of the U.S. markets. While export sales may be a preliminary step to establishing full-blown foreign operations, it must be emphasized that supply and financing benefits may have no relation to the foreign operations in the supplying or financing countries themselves. For the latter, varying international conditions merely represent opportunities to enhance the parent company's worldwide financial strategies.

The third section includes all the vehicles that a multinational company may use to fund and manage cash and capital investments in each foreign country and on a global basis. The goal is to minimize worldwide, consolidated investment levels and their related capital costs to maximize returns on the investment and add to the corporation's overall stock valuation.

The fourth section is aimed at neutralizing what is one of the major annoyances and risks for any U.S.-based corporation doing business with the rest of the world. Foreign exchange rate fluctuations can both directly and indirectly affect the reported results—

through on-balance-sheet assets and liabilities denominated in foreign currencies being consolidated into U.S. dollar financial statements and through both on-balance-sheet rights and obligations denominated in currencies other than those in which the revenues are booked. Foreign exchange, dividend, and other remittance regulations of foreign governments can also reduce the value to the corporation of income generated by foreign operations and exports. Lessening these problems through sound treasury practices allows the corporation to navigate in international waters with more confidence. In fact, many opportunities for profits or savings would not have arisen if foreign exchange transactions were still considered problems—for example, the issuance of foreign currency debt at favorable rates and/or under favorable terms.

Given the basic aim discussed above—namely to serve the international treasury practitioner and investment analyst in their role as members of a company's overall financial management team—this book also incorporates three underlying, pervasive themes:

1. Emphasis on accounting and its effects on the consolidated financial statements;
2. Discussion of the supposedly esoteric international finance phenomena in terms of basic financial concepts taught in basic finance courses;
3. Necessity for a corporate financial game plan, apart from banking and economic criteria, to handle international finance in practice.

The first theme is obvious to anyone who discusses financial ratios from a credit-evaluation or stock-valuation perspective. The starting point is nearly always the consolidated financial statements, and the effects of international financial strategies on these statements must always be fully analyzed.

The second theme concentrates on the extension of international finance beyond basic financial concepts. For example, since inflation and risk are two of the elements that determine interest rates—along with riskless real return requirements—foreign exchange rates can be considered merely a form of interest rate. Of course, uncertainty in exchange rates may be even greater than that in U.S. interest rates, but foreign exchange contracts can be used to manage their effects.

The third theme focuses on specific financial strategies for specific corporate needs. In other words, it is usually not a matter of spotting a good foreign exchange rate or interest rate, but a matter of finding such rates when necessary to carry out the corporation's financial programs.

Therefore, this book should teach the international financial manager or treasury staff member how to answer three major types of questions facing a multinational corporation:

1. How to support prices by participating in the Eurocurrency and foreign capital and supply markets to reduce overall interest costs and/or to obtain favorable terms for debt and equity financing;
2. How to fund foreign operations and manage their excess cash in a manner that optimizes the consolidated corporate financial ratios and stock valuation;
3. How to neutralize or at least dampen the risks of foreign exchange rate fluctuations and blockages that can distort the overall corporate earnings performance and can reduce the value of the corporate stock.

We would be much obliged to receive reactions and suggestions on how the book answers these three major types of questions from financial managers—present or potential—and students and faculty—in both corporate management development programs and universities. Also, we are anxious to hear about where this book can be used as a core text in Executive M.B.A. and non-degree training programs as well as a supplementary text to standard college texts in international corporate finance degree and certificate programs.

S.K. Kaushik
L.M. Krackov

Acknowledgments

We are thankful to Linda Epps, Rebecca Taylor, and Alberta Buchanan for editorial support and Tracy Angerame for research assistance in desktop publishing using Microsoft-Word, Wordperfect, and Xerox Ventura Publisher.

Fred Dahl and Jeanmarie Brusati at the New York Institute of Finance were most helpful in all aspects of publishing this book. Their invaluable assistance as Director of Publishing and Production Editor for the project, respectively, led to the timely and high-quality production, and is most appreciated.

Dr. Carl Crego, Assistant Professor of Finance at Pace University's Lubin Graduate School of Business, read the final copy and made valuable comments.

Pace University provided research assistance and word processing facilities for which we are grateful.

PART I

INTERNATIONAL ENVIRONMENT FOR FINANCIAL DECISIONS

The dynamics of changing economic and financial variables in the international commercial arena today must be monitored continually to make prudent decisions.

In this section, we highlight the importance of the general international economic environment in the late 1980s and beyond. This shows the playing field on which the multinational corporation competes.

This section presents international economic systems and foreign trade in Chapter 1, foreign banking systems in Chapter 2, foreign capital markets in Chapter 3, and Eurocurrency and foreign exchange markets in Chapter 4. Together, these chapters provide the multinational financial manager with the background necessary for the discussion in the next three sections of strategies and decisions that he or she must continuously consider and make.

CHAPTER 1
International Economic Systems and Foreign Trade

Multinational financial management is a development of two types of economic transactions across national borders—real and purely financial. Both types of transactions depend on the economic, financial, legal, political, technological, sociocultural, and foreign trade environment in each country as well as internationally. An understanding of these environments by the multinational financial manager is vital to enable him or her to exploit the opportunities presented by the dynamic growth of the international economy. The relationship between international economic system and financial decision making is discussed here as the necessary foundation for subsequent chapters in this book.

PURPOSES AND BENEFITS OF FOREIGN TRADE

The fundamental reason for foreign trade is the same as that for trade between two economic entities within a domestic economy. Trade or exchange takes place when the entities involved perceive a gain for each side. Conditions for this mutual gain or benefit can vary. For example, at the simplest level, domestic trade or exchange makes it possible for one party to have something that it could not create on its own. Similarly, international trade allows people to acquire things from other countries that they could not or would not make on their own. The fact that people use goods and services produced beyond their national boundaries is obvious proof of mutual gain from international trade. Trade increases the standard of living of both parties. Thus, one purpose of international trade is to increase income (the standard of living) in the countries engaged in trade with each other.

Generally, three situations form the economic basis for trade, and each is progressively more important as a basis for trade and mutual gains to be derived by each party from the exchange.

- **Exclusiveness of a resource, good, or service** can arise due to natural endowments, either physical or human, or knowledge and technology. Countries that do not possess a good can have it by importing from a country that has it. However, if they decide to obtain it, they must pay for it or exchange some other commodity in a barter situation. In other words, trade can make available goods that one does not have but would like to have.
- **Absolute cost advantage** takes the basis for trade a step further. Here, one country can benefit through the trade of a commodity even if the country possesses it, so long as it can be acquired more cheaply elsewhere. The country that has lower costs of producing a good can begin to specialize and produce more of that product to export and thus give the benefit of lower costs to both the importer and itself. The importing country can specialize in something that it can produce more cheaply than another country. The concept of absolute cost advantage opens up the economic reason for exchange—that is, cost—and begins to highlight the importance of *specialization.*

Specialization, through the division of labor, capital, and other resources, leads to further economies and better use of resources. This process of specialization creates other sources of benefits, such as economies of scale and expertise, which in turn reduce the costs of producing increasing amounts of goods and services. The principle of cost advantage thus focuses on the better use or *allocation of resources.*

- **Comparative cost advantage** is the ultimate logical result of seeking economic efficiency or reduction of costs through specialization derived from trade. This principle argues for specialization based on the ability to produce a good more cheaply than another in the same country compared with another country. According to this principle, a country can and should produce more of something even if its costs are only slightly lower for this good versus another good compared with the relative costs of producing these two goods in another country. Thus, the reason for specialization is the slightest of differences in relative costs in the two countries. Simply put, no stone is left unturned to achieve the lowest cost allocation of resources in the production of goods and services. A given bundle of resources thus leads to maximum production (income) and the creation of more resources over time.

Thus, the three basic reasons for trade show that it leads to better (lower cost) use of resources, production of goods and services that a country can produce more of or of better quality, a higher standard of living through more income (production) and consumption, and in turn more trade. The end result is similar to exchange in the domestic economy, where mutually beneficial international exchange increases the incomes and the standards of living of participants in the exchange.

REAL TRANSACTIONS

Until recently, international transactions throughout history were determined by the exchange of real commodities, goods, and services. Metals, raw materials, and food items have been traded throughout recorded history and remain important today. The industrial revolution of the eighteenth and nineteenth centuries increased enormously the exchange of commodities. But the industrial revolution's product—namely, manufactured goods—sought markets throughout the world and thus expanded trade in finished goods. The process of importing raw material and then exporting finished goods in the earlier decades of the first industrial revolution also created a need for exploration, mining, and the trade of more raw materials. The last one hundred years or so witnessed this type of exchange expanding at a very rapid rate.

The birth and growth of modern multinational corporations are the best testament to the process of international trade in raw materials. Trade in manufactured goods achieved high rates of growth in volume only during the post-World War II period—mostly the last 20 or so years.

The multinational corporation uses real transaction trade as both an importer and an exporter. Such trade improves the profitability of its domestic business costs and sales apart from any foreign operations that it may establish, as discussed in Chapter 5.

FINANCIAL TRANSACTIONS

As trade in materials and manufactured goods increased, so did the need for financing. For the most part, financial transactions originated in their counterpart—real transactions. In the last 15 to 20 years, there has emerged a new phenomenon of financial transactions that are not based on real transactions. Today financial transactions dominate international markets. The trade of foreign exchange on a daily volume basis far exceeds the trade of materials and finished goods. Portfolio investments have become global and have spread across the world's financial markets in pursuit of income. This phenomenon is simply an extension of the application of the principle of comparative advantage in resource allocation to its most general level. Technology makes it possible, and economic opportunities for gains and the risk-minimizing behavior of economic entities drive the growth of financial transactions.

Thus, raw materials, finished goods, services, and finance are all exchanged in international markets, where each type of exchange leads to more of others. International exchange yields benefits to and affects the cost of economic laws on the parties to the exchange and effectively renders the world economy a domestic economy, while allowing nation states to remain separate economic, political, and legal entities.

The multinational corporation uses international financial transactions both to obtain funds and to invest excess cash. Such transactions improve the profitability of both domestic and foreign operations, as discussed in Chapters 6, 9, and 10.

INTERNATIONAL ECONOMIC SYSTEM

Two situations have made it possible for world trade in goods, services, and finance to expand to the present levels. One is the recognition that international exchange based on competition among producers across national boundaries is beneficial to each country and its residents. The second is that the setting up of rules of the game for international exchange and the creation of institutions and mechanisms enhance mutual benefits of exchange. There is universal agreement on the first point. However, an ideal environment of rules, institutions, and mechanisms is more difficult to achieve due to the natural tendency to think and behave in terms of national interests which do not always coincide with the terms of exchange.

At the center of the international economic system are the General Agreements on Trade and Tariff (GATT) and some of the key international and regional organizations created to foster international trade and economic growth: the International Monetary Fund (IMF); the International Bank for Reconstruction and Development (IBRD or World Bank), International Development Association (IDA); the International Finance Corporation (IFC); the Bank for International Settlements (BIS); regional development banks such as the Inter-American Development Bank (IDB); the United Nations Conference on Trade and Development (UNCTAD); the Organization for Economic Development and Cooperation (OECD); the European Economic Community (EEC or Common Market); and European Monetary Systems (EMS).

International institutions provide common rules and procedures for international transactions, mechanisms and payments for financing transactions for which private financing is not available or is too costly, and mechanisms for coordination of policies agreed on by the group of countries in the organization. These institutions promote private market transactions in goods, services, and finances and supplement private exchange where needed.

CORPORATE SOURCING OF IMPORTED GOODS

Business enterprises, particularly multinational companies, seek out materials, semifinished products, and capital at the lowest cost. Businesses then transfer these resources to where they can be used as inputs or final consumption items. This process tends to equalize prices. Price signals allow suppliers around the world to produce these resources, goods, and services that businesses order for their worldwide, domestic, or international customers.

Minerals and commodities such as iron ore, oil, copper, wood, cotton, wheat, soybeans, corn, fish, and meat are a large group of resources that businesses transfer from one place to another. Traditionally, the process of industrialization has created such a large demand for these resources that industrialized or developed countries have found it necessary to look for sourcing of such items beyond their home markets. In fact, the import of these commodities has created a whole group of countries described as the Third World; they have a low level of industrialization and earn a disproportionate amount of foreign exchange by exporting commodities relative to finished goods.

Our point here is merely to indicate that a corporate manager is directly involved in making international choices in sourcing of commodities. This decision-making process involves more and more nontraditional imports such as machine tools, specialty labor, and, of course, capital for financing operations in each country and globally through its head office or home office.

Another trend that has emerged in corporate decision making in recent years is the diffusion of activity around the world. Manufacturing, office management, and distribution systems are used in many locations. Unlike the East India Co., which imported cotton from Egypt and India to mills in Manchester, England, modern manufacturing and trading companies locate where it is cheapest to manufacture—not simply where the "home" country is.

Therefore, the international financial manager must be fully at ease in this "international home" to make profit-maximizing decisions and to maximize shareholders' equity in the company. One may be importing a commodity without physically importing it; the processed or manufactured items are imported as inputs or as final consumption items.

We will demonstrate in Chapters 7 and 11 how the aforementioned factors are especially important to the multinational finance manager's approach to capital expansion and repatriation of funds through intercompany sales.

MAJOR MARKETS FOR EXPORT GOODS

A major beneficiary of our open international economic system in the postwar period has been international trade. Success stories of both developed and Third World countries whose international trade (exports) has led to rapid economic growth are many. Exports as engines of growth are commonly accepted by policymakers. This belief is fully supported by the facts as they are collected and analyzed by economists, research groups, and government departments. West Germany, Japan, Taiwan, Korea, Brazil, and India, among others, are examples of countries benefiting from export-led growth.

The international manager is at center stage in this remarkable growth. A more open trading system opens up markets and challenges the enterprise, whether or not the manager wants to get involved. An activist manager can benefit from exports and minimize risks presented by imports in the home market. Therefore, the international manager must maintain the overall picture of the company while focusing on international markets. This holds true for product design, pricing, marketing, distribution, manufacturing location, and, indeed, financing.

The key point to recognize is that trade is a two-way street; when total trade increases, it increases both ways whether one participates in the process or ignores it. Ignoring potential expansion of markets abroad may, and usually does, lead to loss of even the home market. Trade is an activist proposition whether one is defensive in the home market or offensive in foreign markets.

However, exports require a great deal of knowledge and effort. Some areas such as international banking services, foreign exchange markets, and trade mechanisms are presented in more detail in Chapters 2 through 4. Proper use of these markets is presented in Parts II and III.

U.S. TRADE AND PAYMENTS

International trade remained relatively less important in U.S. economic history until the middle of this century. The supreme economic position of the United States in the world economy has been reducing the comfort of an insulated, large, and prosperous industrial society.

The U.S. multinational corporation followed the tradition of its European ancestors in mining and other resource-based industries around the world. Huge direct investment in these activities around the world generated huge imports of these resources. Fed by domestic and imported resources, industrial growth produced high levels of income growth and importing of consumer and producer goods. Due to the open trading system, imports in recent years have ranged between $400 billion and $500 billion a year. These figures translate into about 10 percent of the gross national product (GNP)—not a large percentage by European or Japanese standards, but very large compared with 4 percent or so throughout much of U.S. history.

The U.S. multinational corporation did not do much on the export side. Exports were generated as a by-product of the creation of goods and services for the domestic economy. Until very recently, most of the export industries in the United States were where there were no foreign producers. Foreigners could not meet international demand, or the United States had a unique technological advantage that gave it the benefit of exclusiveness or absolute cost advantage. Food grain, steel, aircraft, chemicals, pharmaceuticals, automobiles, computers, machine tools, heavy earth-moving and construction equipment, farm equipment, military equipment, lumber, and management services accounted for most U.S. exports. But these products sold themselves because of the virtual U.S. monopoly in these industries. Customers came to the United States to order these products. Unlike Europeans and Japanese, U.S. industry did not have to become a traveling salesman to the rest of the world.

But the rest of the world developed its industry in due course and became a salesman to the U.S. consumer and producer. The United States then began to lose not only foreign markets but domestic markets to foreign competition. The result has been a huge trade deficit of $150 billion or so each year in recent years. That is, the ratio of exports to GNP is only 5 percent to 6 percent, leaving a gap of 3 percentage points between imports and exports. This is the power of international trade.

U.S. exports are rising, but it will take a few more years to balance the trade account. U.S. industry is learning fast and catching up with the rest of the world in product development and export promotion. The U.S. manager is now forced to recognize the importance of the international dimension.

Financial markets are in even more turmoil due to large U.S. borrowings from the rest of the world, which have led to deep depreciation of the U.S. dollar in international currency markets. Depreciation is necessary to make foreign goods more expensive to import and domestic goods cheaper to export. Like any price change, the exchange rate change is painful; but this is increasing exports. It is slow but, nevertheless, proceding as expected. What a different story it would have been if U.S. managers of industry had paid more attention to the international dimension in the 1970s!

SUMMARY AND CONCLUSIONS

International trade is beneficial to the world economy—that is, to all participants in the trade process. Trade has led to growth of the world economy faster than it could otherwise have occurred. The multinational financial manager and his or her company must look at both sides of the import-export picture in the corporate decision-making process. U.S. exports must grow to balance the trade account and to stabilize the international exchange value of the dollar. This adjustment puts the burden squarely on the manager, especially the multinational financial manager.

SELECTED REFERENCES

Baldwin, Robert E. and J. David, Richardson, *International Trade and Finance Readings,* Little Brown and Co., Sections I and III and Epilogue, 1974.

Board of Governors of the Federal Reserve System, *Federal Reserve Bulletin* (monthly).

Grennes, Thomas, *International Economics*, Prentice-Hall, 1984, pp.1–645, Chapters 1–5.

Kenen, Peter B., *The International Economy*, Prentice-Hall, 1985, pp.1–552, Chapters 1–4.

Kindleberger, Charles P., and Peter H. Lindert, *International Economics*, Richard D. Irwin, Inc.

Root, Franklin R., *International Trade and Investment*, South-Western Publishing Co., Fifth Edition, 1984, Chapters 11–14 and 21–24.

United States Department of Commerce, *Survey of Current Business* (monthly).

CHAPTER 2

Foreign and International Banking Systems

Multinational corporations have long depended on banking services in their international activities. Banking services are needed for foreign *direct investment* as well as for *portfolio investment* made by corporations.

BANKING SERVICES FOR THE MULTINATIONAL CORPORATION

The role of banking as a source of funds has expanded in recent years. Increasingly, banks not only supply funds and open credit lines, but also act as conduits in facilitating corporate funding in debt and equity markets. Investment banking and merchant banking have thus assumed an increasing share of banking services.

Banking markets have become international in that banks compete among themselves and with non-deposit-taking financial services firms to raise funds and to provide service to multinationals. Competition has also become a reality between banks and their multinational clients' treasury and financial management units.

Multinationals need a number of banking services, or what financial services firms sometimes call products and instruments. Payments and collections, transfers, foreign exchange, credit lines and funding in different currencies, letters of credit, guarantees, references, investment banking, advisory services, and the processing of trade documents are some of the major services that we discuss in Chapters 3 through 6, 9, 10, 13, and 14.

Of course, the globalization of the world economy would not be at the level that it is now, without the efficient banking and financial services that have become commonplace in the 1980s, thanks to computers and telecommunications technology, deregulation, and competition. The evolution of international banking, due to differences in these and fundamental economic factors, has differed across countries. The significant growth of foreign banks operating in the major banking centers can be seen in Tables 2-1 and 2-2.

TABLE 2-1: *FOREIGN BANKS' PRESENCE IN SELECTED COUNTRIES*

Host Country	*1960*	*1985 (end-June)*
Number of institutions in:		
Belgium	14	57
Canada	0	57
Italy	1	36
Netherlands	NA	40
Switzerland	8	119
United Kingdom	51	293
Number of banking offices in:		
France	33	147
Germany	24	287
Japan	34	112
Luxembourg	3	106
United States	NA	783

Source: BIS, *Recent Innovations in International Banking,* April 1986, Table 7.1, p. 151.

TABLE 2-2: *FOREIGN BANKS' ASSETS (percentage of all banks operating in the host country)*

Host Country	*1960*	*1985 (end-June)*
Belgium	8.2	51.0
Canada	NA	6.3
France	7.2	18.2
Germany	0.5	2.4
Italy	NA	2.4
Japan	NA	3.6
Luxembourg	NA	23.6
Switzerland	NA	12.2
United Kingdom	6.7	62.6
United States	NA	12.0

Source: BIS, *Recent Innovations in International Banking*, April 1986, Table 7.2, p. 152.

Cross-border claims among banks in U.S. dollars account for most (about two-thirds) of claims, as can be seen in Table 2-3. However, other currencies are growing in use and they have experienced higher annual growth rates in recent years (Table 2-4).

MAJOR FOREIGN BANKING SYSTEMS

Britain

The British banking system, supervised by the Bank of England, consists of deposit banks, acceptance houses, and other banks, including British overseas banks, merchant banks, and certain finance companies. The system also includes a large number of foreign banks, building societies, finance houses, national savings banks, and trustee saving banks.

The five clearing banks and their subsidiaries (as shown in Table 2-5) with a large branch system, a large number of foreign banks, and discount houses make London the biggest financial center in the world.

The sterling market itself has undergone significant changes.

TABLE 2-3: *INTERNATIONAL BANKING MARKET SIZE (end of period, billions of dollars)*

	Gross Claims (1982–Dec. 1987)		Gross Liabilities (1982–Dec. 1987)	
Claims on and liabilities to Eurocurrencies, residents and nonresidents	2,146	4,405	2,168	4,461
Nonbanks	634	1,284	432	808
Banks	1,512	3,121	1,736	3,653[1]
In dollars	1,694	2,891	1,741	2,924
In other currencies	452	1,515	427	1,537
Domestic currencies, nonresidents	398	915	250	782
Nonbanks	132	222	70	191
Banks	266	693	180	592
In dollars	211	221	116	262
In other currencies	187	694	134	520
Total	2,544	5,320	2,418	5,243
Nonbanks	766	1,506	502	999
Banks	1,778	3,814	1,916[2]	4,244
In dollars	1,905	3,112	1,857	3,186
In other currencies	639	2,209	561	2,057
Net market size	1,285	2,377		

[1]Includes $91 to official monetary institutions in 1982 and $151 in Dec. 1987.
[2]Includes liabilities to official institutions.
Source: World Financial Markets, Morgan Guaranty Trust Co., issue 3, July 1, 1988, p. 15.

For example, foreign banks have made significant inroads into the sterling deposit and loan markets. On the other hand, British clearing banks have a much enhanced role in foreign currency-related business, where they compete with foreign banks. The Banking Act of 1979 and deregulation of the banking and securities markets since then have further established the preeminence of London in international banking.

TABLE 2-4: *GROWTH OF CROSS-BORDER CLAIMS OF BIS-REPORTING BANKS (as a percentage of end-period stocks)*

Currency	*1981*	*1985 (nine months)*
U.S. dollar	12.3	2.9
Deutsche mark	11.8	4.8
Swiss franc	14.7	12.9
Yen	31.6	30.3
Sterling	23.2	13.7
French franc	9.6	14.1
Guilder	19.5	3.7
ECU	NA	48.3
Other	23.0	20.0

Source: BIS, *Recent Innovations in International Banking,* April 1986, Table 7.5, p. 161.

France

The French system in many ways rivals the British system; and in recent years it has been following the deregulation phenomenon in Britain and the United States. Public sector banking institutions and their restrictive practices with regard to maintenance of high liquidity and short-term maturity have somewhat hampered the role of Paris in international banking. Nevertheless, the system, whose center is the Banque de France, consists of registered banks, including deposit banks, investment banks, medium and large credit banks, finance companies, cooperative societies

TABLE 2-5: *CLEARING BANKS AND THEIR SUBSIDIARIES*

Clearing Banks	*Subsidiaries*
1. Barclays Bank	Bank of Scotland
2. National Westminster Bank	Coults & Co.
3. Midland Bank	Clydesdale Bank
4. Lloyds Bank	
5. Royal Bank of Scotland	William & Glyn's Bank

(such as The Crédit Agricole), and independent societies. The "big three" commercial banks are Société Générale, Crédit Lyonnais, and Banque Nationale de Paris. Examples of independent cooperative societies are the Crédit Mutuel and the Crédit Populaire. There are also the Crédit Foncier de France, specializing in mortgage financing; the Crédit National for medium- and long-term industrial credit; the Banque Française du Commerce Extérieur for export-import financing; the Caisse Nationale des Marches de l'Etat for financing and guaranteeing of public works; the national savings bank and ordinary savings banks; the Caisse des Dépôts et Consignations; the Postal and Telecommunication Authority, which offers checking accounts and postal transfer services; Sociétés de Développement Regional for credit to regional companies; and the Institut de Développement Industriel, which finances industry of national importance.

Foreign banks have increased their presence in recent years. They compete in both domestic and international banking business. Foreign banks are quite successful in deposit taking, trade financing, foreign exchange, international payments services, syndicated loans, and the interbank market. The growth in Eurocurrency and Eurobond markets has given a big boost to international banking in Paris.

Belgium

The Belgium banking system has long played an important role in European international banking. The National Bank of Belgium is the central bank, although it is owned equally by government and private shareholders. Other institutions in the system include commercial banks, foreign banks, savings banks, and institutions for medium- and long-term finance, such as the Société Nationale de Crédit à l'Industrie, the Caisse Nationale de Crédit Professionel, the Société Nationale d'Investissement, the Institut de Ré-escompte et de Garantie, and Postal Giro. The "big three" commercial banks are Société Générale de Banque, Kredietbank, and Banque Bruxelles-Lambert. Foreign banks locate in Belgium to meet the needs of their multinational clients, to whom they can render services in their international operations.

Germany

The German banking and financial system consists of the central bank (Deutsche Bundesbank) organized under the Bundesbankgesetz of 1957; commercial banks organized under the Kreditwesengesetz of 1961 and amendments of 1976; mortgage banks organized under the Hypothekenbankgesetz of 1963 and amendments of 1968 and 1974; landesbanks organized under provincial laws; cooperative banks organized under the Deutsche Genossenschaftsbank, amended as of December 1975; joint stock companies organized under the Aktiegesetz of 1965; Fiscusg organized under the Stabilitaetgesetz (Stability Act) of 1967; and stock exchanges organized under the Boersengesetz of 1968 and amendments of 1974.

The *central bank* is independent of the federal government and is the money policy formulation and implementation authority through the banking system. However, supervision of banks is the responsibility of the federal supervisory authority of banks, the Bundesaufsichtsamt fuer das Kreditwesen, which is part of the federal government. The banking authority grants banking licenses and monitors liquidity, capital ratios, and assets and liabilities. It also collects banking statistics and conducts audits.

The banking system itself is divided into categories according to the legal status and activities permitted.

Commercial banks are classified as the "big three" banks (Deutsche Bank, Dresdner Bank, and Commerzbank); regional banks (about 100), classified in terms of geography or type of lending activity; foreign banks (about 100 with approximately 300 offices); and private banks (about 90).

The big three joint stock banks have branches throughout the country. Regional banks specialize in consumer, commercial, mortgage banking, and so on. This group also includes banks that have a national branch system. Foreign banks serve mainly their international customers as they control less than 3 percent of total assets of the banking industry. Private banks play an important role in investment banking and international underwriting, rather than domestic deposit taking and commercial lending.

Savings banks number approximately 600. There are 12 Giro

central banks. Savings banks control the highest percentage of banking assets (about 40 percent) in Germany. They encourage savings and lend small amounts to depositors. Deposits and loans of savings banks tend to be of longer-term maturity. Half of the loans are secured by mortgages. Giros act as regional central banks to savings banks. Giros provide liquidity to savings banks, act as bankers to regional governments, and engage in foreign trade financing and foreign exchange transactions.

Mortgage banks in Germany number about 40 and specialize in lending to local governments and public bodies. They also lend to EEC governments and agencies. Mortgage banks obtain funds in the market through issuance of debentures. Deposits as sources of funds account for less than 50 percent of capital by regulation.

There are also specialized institutions such as the export credit and insurance Ausfuhrkredit-Gesellschaft (AKA), which is a consortium of banks headed by Deutsche Bank. It provides export credit and works closely with the government credit insurance company—Hermes—which guarantees export credit exceeding maturity of two years.

German banks have also set up a liquidity bank: Liquiditaets-Konsortial-bank Gmblt. All types of banks contribute to the capital and can draw on the pool when they face liquidity problems. Likewise, deposit security funds have been created by commercial savings and cooperative banks since no government deposit insurance is provided to nonbank depositors in Germany.

Larger commercial and savings banks in Germany are called universal banks in that they engage in a range of banking activities such as deposit taking, lending (including mortgage lending), investment banking, merchant banking, brokerage investment management and research, foreign exchange, and bullion trade and dealing. In other words, in Germany there is no separation between commercial, savings, and investment banking and underwriting as there is in the United States.

There are also behavioral differences between U.S. and German banks. German banks tend to be more formal, and their protocol procedures are important in building and maintaining relationships. Their emphasis on maintaining high liquidity and safety of assets contributes to a relatively more formalized channel of relationships, unlike the more aggressive and less formal calls by bank representatives in the United States. This point may be of particular interest to a multinational's financial manager in managing funds in the corporation's worldwide activities.

Germany has over 300 foreign banking offices, and as such, it has a major international banking center in Frankfurt. German banks themselves conduct their international banking through their worldwide branch network, subsidiaries in Luxembourg, and, of course, home offices. Foreign banks, however, have a very small (less than 3 percent) share in banking assets in Germany, unlike in the United Kingdom (more than 50 percent) and the United States (about 12 percent). Foreign banks in Germany compete mainly in international banking services for German and foreign business.

Switzerland

Swiss banking consists of national banks, cantonal banks, credit cooperatives, private banks, Swiss-held banks, foreign banks, mortgage bond banks and investment trusts. Since Switzerland does not have separation of banking and securities, national banks engage in a wide range of financial services from deposit taking to fiduciary accounts to securities trading. They make domestic and international commercial and industrial loans. The "big three" commercial banks are Swiss Bank Corporation, Credit Suisse, and Union Bank.

Confidentiality of bank accounts is the most well-known feature of Swiss banking even though it is not a distinguishing feature of Swiss banking since most banking systems provide confidentiality. Violation of secrecy, however, is punishable as a criminal offense by imprisonment and fine. It is the high quality and sophistication of banking services that has made Swiss banks and Switzerland a major financial center.

Swiss banks also have a definite pecking order based upon status and size. The "big three" Swiss banks, for example, are usually part of an underwriting group even if only one of them is the lead bank.

Swiss banks maintain high liquidity in spite of very low reserve requirements and generally minimal regulation of banking. This conservative philosophy has helped the Swiss franc to gain international use as a medium of exchange due to the stable and low-inflation environment, which is a key element of Swiss monetary and economic policies. Competition based on specialization, high liquidity, and the low risk attached to the bank asset portfolio have enabled Swiss banks to expand both in terms of deposits and loans and as intermediaries.

Japan

Japanese banks have emerged as the biggest and most aggressive in international banking in recent years. Japanese banks are in the top 25 banks in the world, with Dai Ichi Kangyo being the largest. A high rate of savings and huge foreign exchange surpluses have enabled Japanese banks to build their balance sheets. They are quite aggressive in branching and deposit taking throughout the world.

Banks in Japan are not allowed to underwrite corporate securities. They have near monopoly at home as dealers in foreign exchange. Foreign banks compete with Japanese banks in Japan on an equal footing in law and regulation, but not in custom or practice, which are based upon relationships. The relationship of Japanese banks and their Japanese corporate customers is probably the strongest of such relationships anywhere in the Western world.

Tokyo, together with London and New York, has emerged as one of the principal global banking centers. Japan's banking system is very similar to the U.S. system, at least in structure and regulations, and it has followed the liberalization of banking and financial services regulations in the United States in recent years.

Canada

Canada's banking system consists of: the Bank of Canada as the central bank, organized in 1934, with functions similar to the Federal Reserve in the United States; trust and mortgage loan companies; credit unions (caisses populaires in Quebec); and sales finance and consumer loan companies. Foreign banks have a major presence in Canada since 1980. Banking liberalizations of 1986 and the U.S.-Canada Free Trade Act of 1988 have further opened financial services in Canada to foreign banks.

Nationwide branch banking has produced six large commercial banks in Canada that dominate banking markets. The advantage of the large size of Canadian banks is not only in domestic markets but also in international banking. The "big five"—Royal Bank, Canadian Imperial Bank of Commerce, Bank of Nova Scotia, Toronto Dominion, and Bank of Montreal—are similar to the large money center banks in the United States in terms of the sophistication and the range of banking services they provide. Financial innovation can be expected by the multinational in dealing with Canadian banks. Canadian banks also tend to be quite competitive in international banking services.

The Netherlands

The banking and financial institutions under the Netherlands' central bank—'De Nederlandsche Bank N.V.—comprising the banking sector are: universal banks, cooperative banks, securities and credit institutions, general savings banks, and mortgage banks. Other institutions include: installment-sales financing institutions, Bank for Netherlands Municipalities, National Investment Bank, Export Finance Company, Netherlands Credit Insurance Corporation, Netherlands Finance, Netherlands Investment Bank for Developing Countries, Netherlands Reconstruction Company, Netherlands Participation Company, the Post Office Savings Bank, and foreign banks.

The Netherlands does not differentiate between commercial, merchant and investment banking, and banks are allowed to branch out throughout the country. They engage in a full range of banking services for domestic and international clients. The "big three" banks are Algemene Bank Nederland, Amsterdam-Rotterdam Bank, and Nederlandsche Middenstands Bank.

Dutch banks have been at the center of international banking activity for a long time and thus have a rich history of banking services. They remain competitive and efficient among large multinational banks from other countries. The Netherlands is an important center of international banking and financial markets as reflected by the presence of large foreign banks and the involvement of Dutch banks in foreign markets. In addition to 50 or so foreign banking institutions operating in the Netherlands, German banks use the Netherlands as their base for booking international credits.

Others

Please note that the real purpose of the foregoing summaries has been to give an overview of differences in national banking systems. The specific material is not as important as the general approach that multinational financial managers use. They must be fully sensitized to the major differences between domestic and international banking services as they deal with banks in the context of multinational business.

There are a number of other important international banking centers that are assuming a greater role as integration of global financial markets occurs. Hong Kong, Singapore, Australia, and Italy are centers that are already playing a significant role in international banking and financial markets. Philippines, Channel Islands, and the offshore banking centers in the Caribbean are others which have played a major role in recycling funds during the 1970s. Financial managers may need to familiarize themselves with these markets and their players to fully benefit in their management of a multinational's credits and cash.

MAJOR DIFFERENCES IN FOREIGN AND U.S. BANKING PRACTICES

Competition among international banks of many nationalities is producing more standardized services for the multinational corporation. At the same time there remain differences among them. Differences in banking practices are based on cultural and economic history as well as attitudes toward risk and time horizons. Some of the notable practices are discussed in this section. The significant implications for the multinational corporation's financing and cash management are related in Chapters 6, 9, and 10.

The following generalizations presented here need not apply to all specific institutions or portfolios:

- **Liquidity** is generally emphasized more by European banks. French and Swiss banks in particular seem to place a higher premium on liquidity than the U.S. banks. Loan-to-deposit ratios are higher for American banks in comparison with European banks. European banks may also require or attempt to obtain higher compensating balances from their borrowers.

- **Risk** is limited more by money center or clearing banks in the U.K., West Germany, and Switzerland. They maintain higher capital ratios, higher margins on loan rates, and have a lower loan loss record in recent years compared with their American counterparts. European banks are also less aggressive in booking loans to build their balance sheets.
- **Maturity** in the shorter range is preferred to long-term maturities by European banks, as a result of the European focus on international trade financing, and this is consistent with their behavior towards liquidity and risk. European banks, for example, have maintained lower exposure in the Third World compared with U.S. banks. They have participated in syndication loans in Eurocurrency markets to the Third World. They have, of course, wide presence in the Third World and have been there much longer but have deemed lending to them more risky than have American banks. Bilateral and multilateral financing of the Third World and debt forgiveness when circumstances demand it is the position European governments have maintained throughout the Third World debt crises of the 1980s. Thus privatization of lending to much of the Third World has not occurred in Europe, whereas reduction in foreign aid and limits on resources of the IMF and World Bank in favor of private bank expansion have been the U.S. position. Trade in financial services in particular, and the service sector in general, is an important issue to the United States in the Uruguay round of General Agreements on Tariffs and Trade.
- **Relationship banking** is perhaps the most important difference, however, for the multinational corporation. The trend towards profit-center banking and the unbundling of services appears to be somewhat more rapid in the United States. Each transaction and each contact may stand more on its own, so overall service from the account representative is becoming less important for some of the largest, most successful U.S. money center banks; though it is less apparent among regional and other banks.

In Europe and Japan, relationship banking still appears to be more emphasized, even among world-class money center banks. In Canada, even the big five seem to lag behind profit-center trends relative to some big money center banks in the United States.

There is also a trend emerging to emphasize either commercial banking or investment banking among major money center U.S. banks. For example, one major New York bank focuses mainly on commercial banking, while increasing its activity in investment banking. Another New York bank primarily engages in investment banking for its clients, who are fewer in number than in the past, but larger in size. As the regulatory limits on various types of banking activities are removed, bank holding companies are allowed to provide new services. There will tend to be more specialization within the broad range of financial services provided by money center banks.

Yet, some banks are returning to emphasizing pure commercial banking with a focus on relationship banking. This is in part a response to rediscovering the importance of a large deposit base following the disastrous consequences of excessive reliance on correspondent banking by Continental Illinois Bank and Trust Company of Chicago and other U.S. banks. Direct and broker-placed deposits have revealed their weakness as a source of deposits in circumstances when there emerge problems with quality of assets financed through borrowed funds under liability management. Asset management and particularly asset-based lending have become popular among U.S. banks as a general trend toward securitization.

- **National banking** is the most obvious difference between foreign and U.S. banks since U.S. banks are not "national" under U.S. federal laws and regulations. Interstate banking, however, is expected to be a formal reality by 1991 in the United States. The key elements of the present check clearing system in the United States are not used in other countries. Lock boxes to accelerate the corporation's collections may be less important when wire transfers are used among a handful of national banks. Remote clearing disbursement to delay loss of value for the corporation on its payables becomes even more meaningless in a national banking system.

There is also the issue of size as it relates to national versus state banking. It is argued that national banking is needed in the United States so that banks can be larger and become similar in size to the Japanese, British, French, and German banks against whom they compete in global markets in banking and financial services. This argument is the industry's version of what academic researchers have found since the 1960s: the United States is an "overbanked" country. In other words, regulatory structure and market conditions have allowed creation of too many banks for the market size. Therefore, there were a large number of bank failures in the 1970s and 1980s.

The new environment of global banking in the electronic age has simply strengthened the argument in the hands of the industry leaders. The Federal Reserve and its boss, the U.S. Congress, have accepted the argument in allowing interstate banking to be phased in by 1991. Suffice it to say here that the United States will have some form of a national banking system, similar to Britain, Canada, and other countries at some point in the future. Whether this will increase size remains to be seen. Further, it should be kept in mind that size in itself does not mean economic efficiency and thus ability to compete with global banks of other nationalities. Product innovation, service, pricing, asset management, etc. are other important factors in enhancing competitiveness.

- **Capital adequacy** is another major difference between U.S. and some foreign banking systems. However, an important development at the international level will change operation: the 12-nation agreement on capital requirements for banks. The agreement, signed on July 11, 1988 in Basel, Switzerland, calls for implementation of capital to equal 8 percent of total risk-weighted assets by 1992. The countries to the agreement are: Belgium, Britain, Canada, France, Italy, Japan, Luxembourg, the Netherlands, Sweden, Switzerland, the United States, and West Germany.

The new uniform capital requirement among the 12 industrial countries will create a level playing field with respect to capital and thus the ability of banks to increase their asset size. Japanese banks, for example, will have to increase their capital substantially more than U.S. banks, and thus may experience a slowing down of their asset growth.

The U.S. banks will also have to increase their capital. The Federal Reserve adopted and approved the new rule for U.S. banks in August, 1988.

FOREIGN BANK ACTIVITY IN THE UNITED STATES

Foreign banks entered the U.S. market in large numbers during the 1970s and 80s. Most countries have their banks present in the United States. Foreign banks control about 10 percent of total U.S. banking assets. In absolute size, foreign bank assets have grown from $24 billion in 1972 to $56 billion in 1975 and to $272 billion in 1988. The structure of assets and liabilities of foreign banks relative to U.S. domestic banks in 1988 is shown in Table 2-6.

Internationalization of U.S. domestic banking has been occurring throughout the twentieth century following the increase in foreign trade and investment in the United States, and the emergence of the U.S. dollar as the key currency in world trade and payments after World War II. Expansion of multinational business in the 1960s, increase in U.S. imports from around the globe, and financial transactions increasing many times the trading volume have been factors in foreign bank presence in the United States.

Foreign banks service their home clients who have economic ties to U.S. markets, help exports to and from their home countries, facilitate transfers and payments, earn valuable foreign exchange, and help companies and countries raise funds in the U.S. money and capital markets. Total size of assets of foreign banks of different nationalities are presented in Table 2-6 (dollar amounts in Table 2-6 are different from those in Table 2-7 due to different coverage), which gives a more specific and better picture of foreign bank activities in the United States.

Foreign banks have used a variety of forms, under the U.S. federal and state laws, to achieve their goals: representative office, subsidiary, branch, agency, and investment company are the vehicles.

TABLE 2-6: *ASSETS AND LIABILITIES OF DOMESTIC AND FOREIGN BANKS IN THE U.S. ON JUNE 8, 1988*[1] *(billions of dollars)*

	Domestic Banks	*Foreign Banks*[2]
Assets		
Loans and securities	2,300	194
Investment securities	495	27
Trading account assets	23	NA
Total loans	1,782	167
Cash assets	193	17
Other assets	123	62
Total assets	2,615	272
Liabilities		
Total deposits	1,973	64
Transactions accounts	595	8
Savings and checkable deposits	545	3
Other deposits	833	53
Borrowings	346	109
Other liabilities	115	96
Total liabilities	2,434	269
Residual (assets less liabilities)	181	3

[1]Excludes assets and liabilities of international banking facilities.
[2]Includes agencies and branches of foreign banks, Edge Act corporations engaged in banking and New York State chartered foreign investment company subsidiaries of foreign banks.
Source: Federal Reserve Statistical Release H-8 (510) of July 5, 1988.

New York, Atlanta, Miami, Houston, Chicago, Los Angeles, and San Francisco have been the locations most preferred by foreign banks. There were over 500 offices of foreign banks in 1988.

For the multinational financial manager, the significant presence of foreign banks in the United States has greatly added to the degree of competition in terms of both banking prices (interest rates, charges, fees, etc.) and services. Managers had traditionally thought of these banks as major concerns relative to their foreign

TABLE 2-7: *FOREIGN BANK ASSETS IN THE U.S. (billions of dollars)*

	End-1986	
	Dollars[1]	*Percent*[2]
Japan	245.4	8.7
Canada	42.4	1.5
United Kingdom	40.6	1.5
Italy	36.4	1.4
Switzerland	24.5	0.9
France	22.4	0.8
West Germany	11.0	0.4
All other countries	103.9	3.8
Total U.S. banking assets of foreign banks	526.6	19.0
Total assets of domestic banking institutions[3]	2285.9	81.0
Total U.S. banking assets[3]	2812.5	100.0

[1]Amounts for each country include the total U.S. banking assets of all banks from that country, namely, the aggregate of assets of their U.S. branches, agencies, bank subsidiaries, Edge Act and Agreement corporations, and New York State chartered investment companies (called Article XII corporations).
[2]Percent of total U.S. banking assets.
[3]Includes the total consolidated assets (domestic and international) of all U.S. banks.
Source: E. Gerald Corrigan, "A Perspective on the Globalization of Financial Markets and Institutions," *Federal Reserve Bank of New York Quarterly Review*, Spring 1987, vol. 12, no. 1, exhibit II, p. 4.

subsidiaries, as discussed in Chapters 9 and 10. Yet, their U.S. presence has greatly increased the focus on the ability of these banks to support domestic U.S. operations, as discussed in Chapter 6.

International banking by domestic as well as foreign banks in the United States has also grown in the form of international banking facilities (IBFs). Total assets of IBFs exceeded $250 billion in early 1988 (Table 2-8).

TABLE 2-8: *ASSETS AND LIABILITIES OF LARGE INTERNATIONAL BANKING FACILITIES (as of March 31, 1988; billions of dollars)*

Assets	
Gross claims on non-U.S. office of establishing entity	73
In dollars	50
In other currencies	23
Total assets other than claims on U.S. offices of establishing entity	180
In dollars	163
In other currencies	17
Total assets other than claims on U.S. offices of establishing entity	253
In dollars	213
In other currencies	40
Liabilities	
Gross liabilities due to non-U.S. offices of establishing entity	118
In dollars	96
In other currencies	22
Total liabilities other than due to U.S. and non-U.S. offices of establishing entity	151
In dollars	131
In other currencies	20
Total liabilities other than due to U.S. offices of establishing entity	269
In dollars	228
In other currencies	41

Source: Federal Reserve Statistical Release G 14 (416) of April 22, 1988.

SUMMARY AND CONCLUSIONS

The multinational corporation enjoys the benefits of global banking in the 1980s. Competition among banks in domestic and international markets provides funding opportunities and efficient services as banks engage in increasingly innovative financial intermediation. Globalization of banking has also created a few major financial centers in the world. This facilitates large volume funding. Specialization and differences in cultures of banking in different countries remain strong within the universal banking services provided by banks of all nationalities. Deregulation and liberalization of banking markets, although at different stages, have become worldwide phenomena leading to more efficient banking markets.

Multinational financial managers have thus gained a wide variety of instruments and markets to choose from. Yet, they must also be aware of the significant differences in regulations, philosophies, and practices that determine the methods and rates for banking services foreign banks provide, both for domestic operations and operation of foreign subsidiaries.

SELECTED REFERENCES

Bryant, Ralph C., *International Financial Intermediation*, Brookings Institution, 1987, Chapters 1–5.

Bank for International Settlements, *Recent Innovations in International Banking*, April 1986, pp. 1–270.

Benedicte Vibe Christensen, *Switzerland's Role as an International Financial Center*, IMF, Occasional Paper 45, July 1986, pp. 1–40.

Dale, Richard, *The Regulation of International Banking*, Woodhead/ Faulkner, 1984, Chapters 1–2.

Deak, Nicholas L. and Joanne C. Celusak, *International Banking*, New York Institute of Finance, A Division of Simon & Schuster, 1984, Chapters 2, 8, and 11.

Drexel Burnham, *International Investment Monthly*.

Euromoney (monthly).

Federal Reserve Bank of Chicago, *Readings in International Finance*, Second Edition, Section IV and VII.

Federal Reserve Bank of New York, *Quarterly Review*.

Federal Reserve System: Purposes and Functions, Board of Governors of the Federal Reserve System, December 1985, Chapters 1, 5, and 7.

Morgan Guaranty Trust Co., *World Financial Markets* (monthly).

Peat, Marwick, Mitchell and Co., *Banking in London*, Third Edition, 1980.

Peat, Marwick, Mitchell and Co., *Banking in the Netherlands*, Oct. 1979.

Peat, Marwick, Mitchell and Co., *Banking in Australia*, 1982.

Peat, Marwick, Mitchell and Co., *Banking in the Philippines.*

Peat, Marwick, Mitchell and Co., *Banking in Canada*, 1981.

Peat, Marwick, Mitchell and Co., *Banking in Luxembourg*, 1980.

Peat, Marwick, Mitchell and Co., *Banking in Channel Islands*, 1981.

Peat, Marwick, Mitchell and Co., *Banking in France*, 1981.

Peat, Marwick, Mitchell and Co., *Banking in Italy*, May 1981.

Peat, Marwick, Mitchell and Co., *Banking in Belgium*, 1980.

Peat, Marwick, Mitchell and Co., *Banking in Hong Kong*, 1981.

Peat, Marwick, Mitchell and Co., *Banking in Singapore*, August 1981.

Watson, Maxwell, Donald Mathiesen Russell Kincaid, and Eliot Kalter, *International Capital Markets*, IMF, Occasional Paper 43, February 1986, pp. 1–125.

CHAPTER 3

Foreign and International Capital Markets

One of the most important developments in the globalization of capital markets has been the opening up of opportunities for corporations to diversify their sources of funds and portfolio investment opportunities. Major corporations have almost unlimited choices of maturities, currencies, denominations, and other terms in foreign and international debt and equity markets. In this chapter we discuss these choices and then demonstrate their use in Chapters 6, 9, and 10.

FOREIGN CAPITAL MARKETS

In recent years, surplus saving units in the form of institutional and individual investors have begun to diversify their investment portfolios more than ever before. International financial intermediation allows investors in one country to invest in securities of any and all countries that permit it. Countries have been removing barriers on capital movements, foreign exchange controls, and foreign investment and have been either eliminating or substantially reducing taxation of income from foreign and international investments. This has created an international environment of efficient allocation of financial resources. Corporations, especially multinationals, are the primary beneficiaries of this international outlook of countries and investors.

Corporations benefit from homemade (treasury) innovations as well as from innovations in new financial products offered by banks, securities firms, and investment banks. Funding needs are met for local (host-country operation), third-country, and home (headquarters) needs. An exact fit is possible between the characteristics of securities and specific needs for funding, which makes it possible for corporations to minimize the cost of capital while achieving the required mix of financing to maximize their return from activities at home and abroad. An understanding of this environment and all the opportunities that it presents to the corporation is of vital importance in a global environment competitive for goods, services, and capital investments.

PRIMARY DEBT MARKET

A corporation can use many instruments in issuing debt. Foreign and international paper (Eurocurrency notes), bank debt, and foreign, international, and Eurobonds have proliferated in recent years.

Once the funding need is determined (domestic U.S. needs are discussed in Chapter 6 and foreign subsidiary needs are discussed in Chapter 9) all of these choices should be examined with respect to capital structure, fixed versus floating rates, currency mix, and maturity. Investor preference at any given time is important in the choice of the market where a debt issue is to be placed. This can then be followed by decisions with regard to other characteristics leading to minimization of the cost of debt. The choice of straight and hybrid securities should likewise be made with respect to minimization of the cost of funds in given markets.

As mentioned earlier, the mobility of surplus funds has opened choices to the international investor on the one hand and the multinational corporation on the other. European markets have been the principal placement outlets for corporations. The volume of Eurobonds, and foreign and international bonds placed in European markets, for example, has grown to $180 billion in 1987. Similarly, Japanese markets have been absorbing large quantities of corporate debt in recent years. Placements in Japan increased to $278 billion by the third quarter of 1987.

The size of the international bond markets is quite significant, with Eurobonds now much more significant than bonds issued by foreigners in countries, as presented in Table 3-1.

The new mutual funds created by financial intermediaries are very attractive to investors. Mutual funds by industry groupings, geographic regions, countries, and risk categories have allowed wide placement of corporate debt instruments.

Corporations have also preferred issuing debt to equity (see the partially related discussion in Chapter 8 concerning foreign subsidiary capital structure), as debt has allowed them more flexibility and control—along with lower interest rates in Japan and Germany. Other economies where international bond issues have been widely successful are the Netherlands and Britain.

TABLE 3-1: *INTERNATIONAL BOND ISSUES (billions of dollars)*

By Type of Instrument and Currency	*1985*	*1986*	*1987*
International bond issues	168	228	177
Eurobonds	137	189	140
U.S. dollar	98	119	57
Japanese yen	7	19	23
Deutsche mark	9	17	16
British pound	6	11	15
Australian dollar	3	3	9
European composite units	7	7	7
Canadian dollar	3	5	6
Other	4	8	8
Foreign bonds	31	39	37
Swiss franc	15	23	24
U.S. dollar	5	7	6
Japanese yen	6	5	3
Other	5	4	4

Source: Morgan Guaranty Trust Co., *World Financial Markets*, issue 3, July 1, 1988, p. 16.

Debt issues have responded to investor preferences with respect to maturity and currency of denomination. The huge success of Euronotes and the commercial paper market in the mid-1980s is a prime example of the globalization of debt securities. The presence of commercial and investment banks from all major economies in these markets, as discussed in Chapter 2 and exemplified in Chapter 6, indicates the importance of the corporate debt market to these intermediaries.

The success of primary debt markets and instruments has also led many experts and practitioners to look for solutions to the Third World's bank debt problems in the bond market. Various types of bond issues are attractive because of the secondary market in debt issues and the continuous adjustment in the market value of debt (unlike the treatment of loans on commercial banks' books). Bondholders are also willing to accept higher risks for expected higher returns. Beyond that, markets make it possible to diversify portfolios and to reduce portfolio risk. The multinational financial manager can and should profit from these markets.

As intermediaries in international capital markets, banks themselves have increased their primary issues. This increase in banks' source of funds can also make their financing more available or affordable to multinational corporations. There has been a dramatic increase in their note and bond issues between 1982 and 1985, as can be seen in Table 3-2.

TABLE 3-2: *SECURITIES ISSUED BY BANKS (billions of dollars)*

	1982	*1985*
Floating rate notes	4.9	29.2
Other bonds	6.1	13.8
Total	11.0	43.0

Source: BIS, *Recent Innovations in International Banking,* April 1986, Table 5.5, p. 139.

PRIMARY AND SECONDARY EQUITY MARKETS

Foreign and international equity markets are also becoming available to corporations. More and more issues are listed on stock exchanges in many countries, which increases liquidity for the investor and makes it possible to issue new equity at lower costs than in purely domestic markets. (See Chapter 6 for a discussion of the U.S.-based multinational's global equity issues.) International diversification of risk is another reason for investor interest in foreign stocks, and this is also being used by multinational corporations for both their own portfolio investments and those of their pension funds.

Mutual funds are one way in which investors around the world can take equity positions in corporations of many different countries. Stock mutual funds have been even more popular in the 1980s than foreign bond funds. There are specialized stock mutual funds according to industry, country, and region. They are further grouped according to risk category. These markets have high liquidity as a result of 24-hour trading done by securities firms. The process of trading is becoming increasingly easy as more and more securities firms become members of stock exchanges in many countries. The London, Toronto, Tokyo, Hong Kong, Frankfurt, Amsterdam, and Sidney stock exchanges are examples of membership by foreign securities firms. These securities firms are not only able to provide 24-hour trading on many stock exchanges, but they are also increasingly able to provide close analysis and advisory services to investors and corporate issuers alike. In capitalization decisions, the corporate financial manager now has more opportunity to benefit from differences in capital markets across countries. Also, global equity issues in all major stock markets at once have expanded the size of the largest stock flotations that can be absorbed by global investors.

More and more foreign stocks are listed on U.S. exchanges, where they are usually traded as American depository receipts (ADRs) based on the underlying shares held in the custody of a bank. ADRs are traded in a manner similar to other shares and offer the same arbitrage opportunities to investors.

International equity markets are also attractive vehicles for funding corporate operations in the economic environment of multicountry subsidiary and joint ventures, along with the traditional direct investment by corporations beyond their home market. Local currency stock issues can supplement bond issues and bank credit lines.

Stock exchanges in different countries have different rules and regulations. There is no single international agency supervising the operation of stock exchanges worldwide. Thus, the multinational financial manager may be able to take advantage of local conditions.

PAYMENTS SETTLEMENT

One clear indicator of the internationalization of financial markets is the daily flow of funds to settle payments. The daily flow through the Federal Reserve Bank of New York exceeds $400 billion. More than half of the total daily flow is accounted for by international payments through the Clearing House Interbank Payments System (CHIPS), as can be seen in Table 3-3.

TABLE 3-3: *FEDWIRE AND CHIPS PAYMENTS FOR PARTICIPANTS BY SIZE CLASSIFICATION ON WEDNESDAY, JUNE 4, 1986*

	1–5 Million Dollars	*5–30 Million Dollars*	*30 Million Dollars and Over*	*Total*
Number				
Fedwire	5,350	4,958	1,528	11,836
CHIPS	16,725	10,642	1,127	28,494
Total	22,075	15,600	2,655	40,330
Amounts (in millions of dollars)				
Fedwire	12,662	61,652	122,729	197,043
CHIPS	35,772	97,232	71,852	204,857
Total	48,434	158,884	194,581	401,900

Source: Staff Report, "Large Dollar Payment Flows from New York," *Federal Reserve Bank of New York Quarterly Review*, Winter, 1987–88, vol. 12, no. 4, Table 2, p. 9.

SUMMARY AND CONCLUSIONS

Foreign and international capital markets are significant sources of funds for the multinational corporation. They also provide a wider opportunity for corporate portfolio investments, both for domestic corporations and foreign subsidiaries.

The growth of the debt market reflects a variety of instruments. Consequently, these markets can match between savers and investors across countries. Electronic payment settlements, usually on the same day, make these markets nearly perfect in terms of information and execution of transactions.

Short-term and long-term debt has been the source of funds preferred by issuers in international markets. Yet stock exchanges are now linked worldwide, and 24-hour trading is in place in major markets. Increasing numbers of stocks are listed on many stock exchanges, making it possible for investors in various markets to provide more liquidity, depth, and width in equity markets.

Multinational financial managers must stay close to developments in these markets to insure that optimal corporate financial strategies are being employed for their corporations.

SELECTED REFERENCES

BIS, *Innovations in International Banking*, April 1986.

Deak, Nicholas and Joanne C. Celusak, *International Banking*, New York Institute of Finance, A Division of Simon & Schuster, 1984.

Drexel Burnham, *International Investment Monthly*.

Euromoney (monthly).

Federal Reserve Bank of Chicago, *Readings in International Finance*, Second Edition.

Federal Reserve Bank of New York, *Quarterly Review*.

Morgan Guaranty Trust Co., *World Financial Markets* (monthly).

Strongin, David G., "We will meet at the Plaza," *International Capital Markets Review*, vol. III, no. iii, February 16, 1988, pp. 6 and 9.

CHAPTER 4

Eurocurrency and Foreign Exchange Markets

Eurocurrency markets and their growth are at the center of the globalization of banking and capital markets. Before the emergence of the Eurodollar market in the late 1950s and its phenomenal growth during the 1960s and 1970s, international banking was essentially limited to payment services, lending to foreign borrowers from the home office, and, sometimes, the establishment of foreign branches. The Eurodollar market and markets in other currencies outside the home of the currency have changed the character of international banking and finance.

INTERBANK MARKET

At its core, the Eurocurrency market is the interbank market in deposits and lending. The core interbank deposit amount in all currencies is estimated to be around $1,000 billion ($1 trillion). About two-thirds of this is in U.S. dollars, with the balance in other currencies, such as the British pound sterling, German mark, Japanese yen, French franc, and others.

EURODOLLAR MARKET

There are many reasons behind the emergence, growth, and dominance of the Eurodollar market in the Eurocurrency market:

- **Use of the U.S. dollar as a reserve currency** by the central banks under the Bretton Woods system;
- **Its use as the currency of denomination** in private international transactions, along with the pound sterling and the limited use of a few other European currencies;
- **The shortage of international liquidity;**
- **The acceptance of dollar deposits first by Britain and subsequently by continental European countries** following the Soviet Union's decision to transfer dollar holdings from New York to London.

In terms of the development and rapid growth of the Eurodollar market, the absence of regulations and reserve requirements gave a big boost to Eurodollar deposits since banks could offer marginally higher interest rates. The overnight Eurodollar market soon became a much larger version of the federal funds market in the United States. The same economic factors made it possible for banks engaged in the Eurodollar market to offer lower interest rates on loans. Thus, the Eurodollar market increased the international liquidity of banks. Soon the activity spread to offshore centers such as the Bahamas, the Cayman Islands, Panama, and so on. The two oil price hikes by the Organization of Petroleum Exporting Countries (OPEC) in the 1970s and their preference for depositing oil revenues in U.S. dollars into short-term bank accounts, usually outside the United States, further boosted the Eurodollar market.

Banks did an excellent job as intermediaries in lending these Eurodollar deposits to government and private borrowers in Europe and increasingly to the Third World countries of South America, Africa, and so on. Upholding the tradition of short-term commercial lending, bankers lent for short-term maturities with risk-adjusted margins over their deposit rates.

The Eurodollar market has served savers, banks, and borrowers in the international community. It has provided both liquidity for the financial system and credit to borrowers for economic activity in the real sector involving trade, investment, and consumption spending. Thus, it has greatly contributed to economic growth. In addition to this efficient intermediation, the Eurodollar market also led to the development of Euro markets in other currencies and in a myriad of maturities and risk categories.

Debt Instruments

During the early 1980s, Eurodollar bonds and floating rate notes emerged as the most successful debt instruments in the Eurocurrency markets. As can be seen in Table 4-1, floating rate notes increased from $12.4 billion in 1982 to $47.8 billion in 1985, while fixed rate straight bonds increased from $19.0 billion to $43.7 billion during the same period. Financial intermediaries also created and placed in the market for their clients convertible bonds, which increased from $1.2 billion in 1982 to $3.8 billion in 1985.

Eurobond issues have continued their growth in recent years with the help of major investment banking firms in all the major money centers of the world. A list of the top 20 underwriters, with their corresponding amounts, is presented in Table 4-2. Firms from France, Germany, Japan, and the United States are the leading underwriters of Eurobonds. The amounts shown in Table 4-2 just for the top 20 firms approach $60 billion in the first half of 1988.

The important point to note about Tables 4-1 and 4-2 is that multinational financial managers are taking full advantage of the Eurobond market by issuing securities through their top international investment bankers from many countries.

The U.S. dollar remains the main currency of denomination

TABLE 4-1: *EURODOLLAR BOND ISSUES (billions of dollars)*

Instrument	*1982*	*1985*
Floating rate notes	12.4	47.8
Fixed rate straight bonds	19.0	43.7
Convertible bonds	1.2	3.8
Total	40.9	95.3

Source: BIS, *Recent Innovations in International Banking*, April 1986, Table 5.3, p. 135.

TABLE 4-2: *RANKING OF EUROBOND UNDERWRITERS (January 1 to June 10, 1988)*

	Firm	*Amount (in billions of dollars)*
1.	Nomura Securities	8.0
2.	Credit Suisse First Boston	7.2
3.	Deutsche Bank	6.8
4.	Daiwa Securities	4.8
5.	Nikko Securities	3.7
6.	Yamaichi Securities	3.4
7.	S.G. Warburg	3.2
8.	Union Bank of Switzerland	3.1
9.	J.P. Morgan Securities	3.1
10.	Merrill Lynch Capital Markets	2.7
11.	Bankers Trust International	2.5
12.	Bankque Paribus	2.5
13.	Goldman, Sachs International	2.1
14.	Commerzbank	2.0
15.	Swiss Bank Corp. Investment Banking	1.9
16.	Morgan Stanley International	1.7
17.	Industrial Bank of Japan	1.7
18.	Salomon Brothers	1.5
19.	Dresdner Bank	1.4
20.	Hambros Bank	1.2

Source: The New York Times, Business Day Section, "U.S. Firms Drop in Rank Among Eurobond Underwriters," July 11, 1988, p. D1.

in both the Eurobond and floating rate note markets, and is dominant in the latter. Yet, there has been a significant increase in the use of the pound sterling and other currencies in recent years (Table 4-3). Sterling and other currencies now account for 20 percent of the Euronote market.

The U.S. dollar is also the leading currency of denomination in international fixed rate bond issues, but it is less dominant than in the floating rate market. The U.S. dollar is used only 44 percent, and other currencies have gained market share since 1982 compared with the U.S. dollar (Table 4-4). It seems that there are more diversified issuers in fixed bonds, as more multinationals from different countries enter the market with their issues, compared with the floating rate note market (Table 4-3), where only the major

TABLE 4-3: *CURRENCIES USED IN INTERNATIONAL FLOATING RATE NOTE ISSUES (percentages)*

Currency	*1982*	*1985 (second half)*
U.S. dollar	98	80
Swiss franc	98	—
Sterling	—	8
Other	1	12

Source: BIS, *Recent Innovations in International Banking*, April 1986, Table 7.6, p. 163.

multinationals can gain financial terms better than credit lines at banks.

Another instrument that has grown rapidly in Eurocurrency markets in recent years is the Euro commercial paper. Euro commercial paper is heavily subscribed by money market mutual funds. Many of the major U.S. money funds invest in Euro commercial paper. Investments of the larger U.S. money funds in Euro commercial paper as a percentage of their assets and as a percentage of their commercial paper portfolios on different dates in 1986 is shown in Table 4-5. The data in Table 4-5 indicate both the significant role investors in the U.S. money market, through the institution of mutual funds, are playing in the Euro commercial paper market and the degree to which they are attaining diversification through this short-term market in their portfolios.

Perhaps more important from our perspective, on the other side of the market are the issuers of Euro commercial paper—

TABLE 4-4: *CURRENCIES USED IN INTERNATIONAL FIXED RATE BOND ISSUES (percentages)*

Currency	*1982*	*1985 (second half)*
U.S. dollar	54	44
Swiss franc	20	15
Deutsche mark	10	8
Yen	7	13
Sterling	3	2
Guilder	3	2
ECU	2	6
Other	1	10

Source: BIS, *Innovations in International Banking*, April 1986, Table 7.3, p. 158.

TABLE 4-5: *FOREIGN COMMERCIAL PAPER HELD BY TOP TEN MONEY MARKET MUTUAL FUNDS INVESTING IN COMMERCIAL PAPER*[1]

	Foreign Commercial Paper:	
	As Percent of Assets	*As Percent of Total Commercial Paper*
Merrill Lynch CMA Money Fund As of March 31, 1986	1.7	6.0
Merrill Lynch Ready Assets Trust As of June 30, 1986	2.7	3.9
Dreyfus Liquid Assets As of March 12, 1986	14.2	68.7
Dean Witter/Sears Liquid Assets Fund As of February 28, 1986	0.4	0.7
Fidelity Cash Reserves As of November 30, 1986	19.8	51.8
Temporary Investment Fund As of September 30, 1986	2.2	2.3
Cash Equivalent Fund-Money Market Portfolio As of July 15, 1987	27.7	37.1
Institutional Liquid Assets-Prime Portfolio As of December 31, 1986	0.0	0.0
Prudential Bache Moneymart Assets As of December 31, 1986	12.1	19.6
Kemper Money Market Fund As of July 31, 1986	34.0	36.7
Total top ten	8.8	16.3

Two funds in the top ten, the Trust for Short-Term Government Securities and the Trust of U.S. Treasury Obligations are specialized funds that invest only in specific government-backed paper.

Source: Robert N. McCauley and Lauren A. Hargraves, "Eurocommercial Paper and U.S. Commercial Paper: Converging Money Markets?" *Federal Reserve Bank of New York Quarterly Review*, Autumn 1987, vol. 12, no. 3, Table 1, p. 26.

namely, the multinational corporation. They are increasing their participation in addition to foreign governments and banks.

In Tables 4-1 through 4-5 and in Chapters 6, 9, and 10, we see that the multinational financial manager is borrowing and investing in all maturity and risk segments of the Eurocurrency market: the Eurobond market, the floating rate market, and the Euro commercial paper market. These borrowings and investments are mainly in the Eurodollar parts of these markets, as the U.S. dollar remains the key currency in these markets.

It is noteworthy that the multinational financial manager is maintaining full flexibility in these markets. For example, the financial manager is using more and more of the various Eurocurrency debt markets, but is still maintaining and utilizing bank credit lines, especially where necessary for timing. Also, bank lines are often maintained in different currencies, which helps in managing cash, foreign exchange, and trade financing.

THE FOREIGN EXCHANGE MARKET

The foreign exchange market is where one currency is traded or exchanged for another. Transactions to exchange currencies are either on the spot market (delivery within two days) or the forward market (delivery on a specified future date). Practically, however, immediate to seven-day delivery is considered by participants to be in the spot market. Pricing, that is, the exchange rate, depends on the delivery date or "value date."

The foreign exchange market is needed to settle payments for the exchange of goods and services, capital investments in another country, or portfolio investments by residents of one country in another. Regardless of the currency of invoice, it is necessary to convert one currency into another to settle payments.

Naturally, the foreign exchange market has grown with the increase in foreign trade, direct investments, and financial transactions involving portfolio investments, speculation, and arbitrage, as well as hedging transactions, in different currencies. The daily volume of foreign exchange transactions in New York alone is estimated to be more than $400 billion in 1988—a sum equal to about 10 percent of the annual GNP of the United States.

Anyone who buys and sells currencies is a participant in the foreign exchange market. Since banks provide the payments mechanism between residents of different countries, they are one of the key players. Banks enter the market on behalf of their clients in many countries and on their own behalf as financial intermediaries. The interbank market in foreign exchange is huge, as it allows banks to balance their foreign exchange positions at the desired level. Other major players are large corporations engaged in multinational activities and, of course, central banks that manage their national currencies and their international or foreign exchange value.

Corporate participation in the foreign exchange market occurs in the form of international capital investment (Chapter 7), import-export activities (Chapter 5), and financing decisions (Chapters 6 and 10). Currency needs—today or in the future, whether for payments settlement, the hedging of currency and foreign exchange positions, or capital investment—bring multinational corporations into the foreign exchange market on a continuous basis (see Chapters 11, 12, and 13).

Central banks enter the foreign exchange market to manage their domestic monetary policy and to influence the foreign exchange rate of their currency in the interests of their domestic economy. Intervention in the foreign exchange market to stabilize the value of a currency may or may not be effective in the achievement of national economic goals. Nevertheless, central banks and treasuries are major players in the market.

FOREIGN EXCHANGE RATES

Foreign exchange rates are a product of supply and demand of the currencies in international markets. Supply and demand of currencies are affected by foreign trade, direct investment and financial transactions, and expectations of the economy's performance as represented by the currency. There are several theories about the determination of exchange rates for a currency in relation to other currencies, but they fall into two main categories:

- **The purchasing power parity theory** focuses on the purchasing power of a currency in its home market and, by extension, in the international market. It assumes there are no restrictions on trade and capital is free to move between countries. The purchasing power of a currency in terms of goods and services should be the same everywhere, whether in its own units or in units of another currency after foreign exchange conversion. The conversion or exchange rate will equalize the purchasing power. Therefore, if domestic prices of goods and services such as the wholesale price index change, this change will be reflected in the exchange rate. If markets are perfectly competitive, with full information about both economies in both economies, an increase in inflation will reduce the value of currency in the foreign exchange market so that the real exchange rate remains the same.

This concept is critical to the major business and financial decisions of the multinational corporation. We discuss this concept in relation to the evaluation of foreign investment cash flows in Chapter 7. It is also closely related to, and underlies the concept of, interest rate parity, which in turn underlies the forward markets used to hedge foreign currency exposures, as discussed in Chapter 13.

- **The balance of payments approach** to determination of the exchange rate views the trading account and short-term financial transactions as generating supply and demand of foreign exchange for a currency. These transactions—not the rest of the economy—and the supply and demand for exchange that they generate principally determine the exchange rate. The balance of international transactions considered is the current account, that is, the net balance for goods, services, and unilateral transfers of funds. Thus, if a country has a deficit, its currency will depreciate as there is a shortage of foreign currency in relation to demand for it by the deficit country. To acquire foreign currency, the deficit country will have to pay more units of its currency for each unit of foreign currency.

In recent theories, financial transactions and expectations regarding the behavior of economies and, therefore, the exchange rate have determined exchange rates. These are extensions of the balance of payments approach, with a focus on financial variables. According to this view, the premium or discount market that participants are placing on the course of the exchange rate in the future when they will receive or make payments are the key factors influencing financial transactions.

The important points for the financial manager are that each transaction in international markets creates a foreign exchange position and that the risk associated with that is to be covered (see Chapter 7) lest one become an unwitting speculator in the foreign exchange markets.

BANK CUSTOMER FOREIGN EXCHANGE MARKET

The bank customer market is, of course, the key market of interest to the multinational financial manager. Banks conduct foreign exchange transactions for their corporate customers at competitive rates, and financial managers must create banking relationships to be able to acquire and manage foreign exchange at the lowest prices.

The key concern of multinational financial managers is their ability to access the worldwide currency markets for three primary purposes. First, they need the efficiency of forward contracts that are cheap (low spreads and bank profits) to cover the foreign currency exposure connected with their company's import-export and foreign subsidiary activities, as discussed in Chapter 13. Second, they need the efficiency of the spot market to make cross-payments for their foreign subsidiaries and domestic operations, as discussed in Chapter 11. Third, they want to maximize their returns on portfolio investments without incurring exchange rate risk, as discussed in Chapter 6.

SUMMARY AND CONCLUSIONS

Eurodollar and other Eurocurrency markets and their growth are one of the most significant innovations in international banking and in financial markets over the past two decades.

The Eurodollar market is still the main segment of overall Eurocurrency markets. Euro markets in other currencies are growing, however, reflecting their use as currencies of invoice based on the underlying economies of Japan, Germany, France, Britain, Switzerland, and the Netherlands.

Euro markets provide the medium for financing sources that supply the multinational corporation and for investment opportunites absorbing portfolio investments of the multinational corporation's excess cash. This is true in the parent's home country as well as the corporation's foreign operations around the world. The multinational should use Euro markets as well as "friendly banks" whenever and wherever possible to achieve corporate goals.

The foreign exchange market may play an even more crucial role in the financial life of a multinational as soon as it steps out of its home market and home currency. The growth of the foreign exchange market reflects growth in trade and payments as well as in financial transactions. The foreign exchange rates follow the purchasing power parity in the long run. Real as well as financial variables play an important role in determining the foreign exchange rates in the short run. Multinationals can use the foreign exchange market to achieve a perfect hedge for their financial transactions unless, of course, they want to take an open (speculative) position, whether consciously or unwittingly speculative. (Appropriate foreign exchange hedging strategies are discussed more fully in Chapter 13).

SELECTED REFERENCES

BIS, *Innovations in International Banking,* April 1986.

Drexel Burnham, *International Investment Monthly.*

Euromoney (monthly).

Federal Reserve Bank of Chicago, *Readings in International Finance*, Second Edition, Section VI.

Federal Reserve Bank of New York, *Quarterly Review*.

Krueger, Anne O., *Exchange Rate Determination*, Cambridge Universtiy Press, 1983, pp. 1–218, Chapters 3 and 4.

Morgan Guaranty Trust Co., *World Financial Markets* (monthly).

Riehl, Heinz and Rita M. Rodriguez, *Foreign Exchange and Money Markets*, McGraw-Hill, 1983, pp. 1–453, Chapters 1–3.

Sarver, Eugene, *The Eurocurrency Market Handbook*, New York Institute of Finance, A Division of Simon & Schuster, 1988, pp. 1–384, Chapters 5–9.

PART II

UTILIZATION OF INTERNATIONAL MARKETS TO SUPPORT DOMESTIC OPERATIONS

The first group of multinational corporation financial decisions to be impacted by the international environment, described at length throughout Part I, concern the parent company's own domestic businesses. As both an importer and an exporter, a company can improve its domestic operations. As both a borrower and an investor, a company can improve its total domestic financial returns compared with its cost of funds to increase the value of the company.

Therefore, this section is conveniently broken into two groups of potential benefits. Import and export opportunities, risks, and safeguards are discussed in Chapter 5. International financing sources and money market investment instruments are outlined in Chapter 6.

While the multinational firm has or is seeking foreign business operations, the utilization of international markets is not limited to such companies. There are many purely domestic U.S. corporations that are major players in the international materials, capital, and money markets. Also, most major U.S. companies with or without foreign operations are significant customers of one or more of the major foreign banks with a strong presence in the United States.

Yet, greater involvement in any foreign or international business markets often broadens the horizons of all senior management decisions. This should make most multinational corporations even more aware of and willing to participate in the various international markets to benefit their domestic businesses and their companies overall.

CHAPTER 5

Benefits and Risks of Import-Export Operations

Multinational corporations establish foreign operations for manufacturing, importing resources to domestic operations, and exporting domestic products to foreign markets. Each of these dimensions of a multinational's life may lead to many other activities and subsidiaries relating to marketing, financing, acquisitions, and so on. Generally, all these aspects should be part of the corporation's strategy. Yet, sometimes import-export operations grow out of unexpected situations, such as when the host country experiences a lack of funds and therefore forces the multinational not only to trade in goods and services not part of its business but to barter. For example, many corporations became involved in barter trade when developing countries experienced a shortage of foreign exchange in the 1982–1985 period.

BENEFITS OF IMPORT OPERATIONS TO SUPPLY THE CORPORATION

Multinational corporations can benefit from sourcing of raw material and components from other countries. Resources may be cheaper in foreign countries where the multinational has a presence in either the same or another industry. Importing of resources is quite often a necessity due to the uniqueness of a resource or its relative scarcity. Plentiful supply in foreign countries may also make resources very cheap, as can lower labor costs and specialized technology. Importing of resources under these conditions reduces production costs at home while also giving the longer-term benefit of a diversified and more reliable supply. The corporation is more able to compete effectively in the market for its product at home and abroad due to lower costs. By importing resources, the corporation eliminates the comparative advantage held by a foreign country based on abundance of resource endowment. Thus, the corporation transfers the benefit to itself and its home country.

The importing of components has assumed greater significance as a device for cost cutting, given big differences in labor costs and in capital/technology requirements for different products and industries. Component manufacturing in different countries for assembly at a few regional centers that the multinational establishes—by itself or through joint ventures with companies already located in these other countries—have expanded importing to supply multinationals at all stages of the production cycle, along with traditional raw materials. In other words, the comparative cost advantage in materials, manufacturing, and assembly is now applied to many micro-parts of a multinational's operations—not just in the macro-comparison of costs across countries. Each part and subpart of the multinational operation follows its own comparative cost advantage. Therefore, importing to supply multinationals has become essential in this new environment of enhanced competition in world trade. Technology, the liberalization of trade, and micro-specialization make resource and component supply at the lowest possible costs critical for today's multinational corporation.

BENEFITS OF EXPORT OPERATIONS TO EXPAND THE CORPORATE REVENUE BASE

U.S. domestic markets were once considered too big to worry about building exports to the rest of the world. However, non-U.S. multinationals always recognized the importance of exports—not only because their home markets were relatively small, but because they saw exports as a source of increased revenues and profits. Western European countries, Japan, and other countries provided clear, long-term support for export-led growth of their economies. This "export mindset" is now spreading among U.S. multinationals, small- and medium-sized companies, and financial institutions.

Part of the importance of exports to enhance the corporate revenue base also derives from the fact that foreign multinationals are competing with U.S. multinationals in their home market. Without belaboring the point, markets for resources are also markets for products. After all, both sides of the import-export coin are important to the multinational by its very nature.

The establishment of import-export operations and their benefits should be decided on the incremental cost and revenue basis. Furthermore, as stated earlier, incremental cost and revenue analysis should be done for each product, service, and its parts so that the benefits are truly attributable to specific import-export activities.

RISKS AND PROCEDURAL PROBLEMS FOR THE CORPORATION AS AN IMPORTER AND EXPORTER

There are always risks involved in business, especially if the new business activity is not part of the multinational's main business. Risks come from the pricing of imports and exports, foreign exchange, the reliability of supply sources, market penetration for exports, cost overruns due to rapid expansion, and the inability to create appropriate new products in the face of increasing competition. Many of these aspects are covered in Chapters 11 through 14.

Also, international trade procedures are the practical aspects of import-export operations involving trade practices, documentary evidence, customs, and so on—to handle credit risks that are discussed in the next section. A multinational may develop in-house expertise in these functions or may utilize specialists as agents. Banks, shipping companies, and customs brokers are always eager to provide their specialized services and should be utilized if they are cheaper than home services.

An additional focus should be kept on the aspects of import-export activities that affect financial transactions of the multinational in its treasury and funds management area: costs, revenues, intercompany transactions, transfer pricing, capital investments, cash management, and their management utilizing banking and foreign exchange markets. These effects and strategies are discussed in Chapters 6, 9, and 10.

INTERNATIONAL TRADE PROCEDURES AND OTHER MECHANISMS TO MANAGE CREDIT RISK

There are inherent credit risks in international trade. These risks relate to performance of contractual obligations on the part of the buyer and the seller. Contractual obligations regarding the terms of contracts involve credit availability, the shipment of goods, the transfer of rights, and the method and timing of payment.

The International Chamber of Commerce (ICC) has developed Uniform Customs and Practices for documentary credits (UCP). The latest revision, which became effective on October 1, 1984 and was accepted by banks in 156 countries, is the general method used in international trade. It allows goods to be shipped and payment to be received by a seller against documents representing the goods upon the transfer of rights to the buyer. The UCP is an attempt to reduce or eliminate the risks listed above. It involves banks and their credit and payment services to settle payments for international commercial obligations. In UCP, a bank undertakes to pay the seller upon presentation of documents stipulated in the undertaking.

This greater credit risk involved in most international trade transactions comes from a lack of familiarity between the two parties in different countries and with each of the other country's restrictions. Banks with which they are familiar are, therefore, added to the deal structure to insure proper payment. Banks also check detailed documents related to the transaction and this acts as a safety procedure for the parties involved. These procedures can insure payment upon delivery to avoid credit risk, delayed payments, and, perhaps, government restrictions.

There are several types of bank documents involved in these credit safeguard procedures:

- **A commercial invoice** includes a description of the merchandise (such as weight, number of packages, quantity, price, terms of delivery and payment, and additional details) and the name and address of the buyer and the seller. The invoice is made by the seller and addressed to the buyer; through it, the seller charges goods to the buyer.
- **A certificate of origin** provides evidence of the origin of goods. It is issued by an independent body such as a chamber of commerce in the country of the seller (exporter). It provides details of the shipment and its origin.
- **A transport document** is the most important document in the documentary credits required by a bank. It shows that goods of a certain description have been shipped by the seller with all the details about place, time, payment, carrier, payment of freight, description of goods, name of the order (buyer or consignee), and so on. Depending on the mode of transport, the appropriate document could be a postal receipt, a marine bill of lading, a combined bill of lading, an air waybill, a road or railway consignment note, an inland water waybill, or an ocean waybill. The transport document contains all the information given on a commercial invoice: information about the carriers, the place and time of dispatch or loading on board, the name of vessel, the final destination, the condition of goods, the shipper, freight, the number of originals of the document itself, and the date of issuance.
- **An insurance certificate** covers risks during transportation in an amount at least equal to cost, insurance, and freight value of the goods plus ten percent in the currency of invoice. It covers goods from the day of shipment and should be consistent with the invoice and the transportation document. The document is issued by an insurance company or its agents. The insurance document must be as specified by the bank in the letter of credit.

- **A letter of credit** by a bank is the actual credit protection issued to the seller (exporter) at the request of the buyer (importer) upon conclusion of a contract between the buyer and the seller. The buyer requests the bank to issue a letter of credit to the seller (beneficiary)—usually because the seller demands this from the buyer—in a specified amount and with the following terms: the type of credit (i.e., revocable, irrevocable, or confirmed irrevocable), settlement of credit by payment, deferred payment, acceptance, or negotiation. The buyer also supplies information to the bank about the party on which drafts are to be drawn; a description of goods, including the quantity and unit price; the payment of freight; documents required; places of dispatch (loading) and final destination; information on transshipment; partial shipments; the latest date for shipment; the period of presentation of documents; the date and place of expiration of the credit; whether the credit is transferable; and the method of advisement of credit.

  Revocable credit may be amended or canceled before the documents are presented for payment, payment has been made, or documents have been taken up for deferred payment. This type of credit still exposes the seller to the possibility of being forced to obtain payment directly from the buyer.

  Irrevocable credit cannot be amended, but still leaves the seller dependent on the importer's bank in a foreign country.

  Confirmed irrevocable credit gives full protection to the seller, as the "nominated" or advising (usually also settlement) bank in its own country—quite likely the exporter bank—confirms the availability of credit upon receipt of advice from the issuing bank.

The draft drawn on the advising (nominated) bank is a different instrument from the letter of credit; it is an order to the bank on which it is drawn to make payment to the seller (beneficiary). The draft can be a sight draft or a negotiable draft. Payment on a sight draft is made on presentation whereas payment on a negotiable draft is negotiated between the seller and the bank.

In practice, the difference between irrevocable credit and confirmed irrevocable credit is that in the former, when the advising bank forwards the original letter of credit to the seller, it sends either a standard notification letter or a notification letter that confirms availability of credit. The standard notification letter is called an acceptance credit, which means that it is available when the seller draws a draft on the advising (nominated) bank. The draft stamped "accepted" becomes a banker's acceptance. The banker's acceptance is then traded (discounted and rediscounted) until the payment date, when the holder of the acceptance collects payment. On the other hand, the confirmed irrevocable credit is called a payment credit and is available to the seller upon presentation of documents specified in the letter of credit within and by the specified date of credit availability.

Settlement itself can be by (1) payment to the seller by the bank on presentation of documents, (2) acceptance of the draft by the advising/confirming bank and return to the seller (or sending to the issuing bank, different from the advising bank, for reimbursement to the confirming bank at maturity of the draft), (3) negotiation of a draft drawn on the buyer or other drawee specified in the letter of credit (at sight or tenor, as specified in the letter of credit). Negotiation by the issuing or confirming bank is without recourse to the seller. Negotiation by a bank other than the issuing and confirming banks is with recourse to the seller. The negotiating bank then receives reimbursement from the issuing bank.

Other types of credits used in international trade are:

- **Revolving credit** can be in relation to time or value and can be revocable or irrevocable. It can also be cumulative or noncumulative. A certain fixed amount of credit is renewed under this type of credit arrangement. For example, the issuing bank makes credit available to the seller every month. A noncumulative credit, if not utilized, expires at the end of the month. A cumulative credit is carried over by the amount of the balance not utilized in a given month and added to the final month, as specified in the terms and conditions of the credit.
- **Red clause or special credit** allows the advising or confirming bank to make payment before presentation of documents so that the exporter has funds before shipment. These funds may, in fact, be used to make the shipment to the buyer. The buyer is in effect financing the seller's operations.

- **Transferable credit** can be transferred by the first beneficiary/seller in favor of the second beneficiary. The credit can be transferred only between the seller and the beneficiary designated by the seller. Only an irrevocable credit can be transferred. Usually this type of credit can be transferred once. The transfer is effected at the request of the first beneficiary to the bank where credit is available. This type of credit arrangement allows the first beneficiary to substitute for its invoice and draft those of the second beneficiary. The bank, of course, makes certain that information on the invoices and other documents submitted by the two beneficiaries are identical and that they meet the terms of the original credit before it makes payment.
- **Back-to-back credit** is arranged when the issuing bank provides credit to the buyer as well as to the seller who has to make payment to a third party. If the issuing bank does not do this, the seller can arrange for its own bank to issue second credit, in which case it becomes *counter credit*. The seller, in a back-to-back credit arrangement, offers the credit available to it as a security to the advising bank against the second credit. Thus, the seller remains responsible for payment to the bank regardless of whether it is paid or not by the beneficiary of the second credit. In a counter credit arrangement, the seller requests its own bank to issue the second credit as a counter to the first one. This is usually done when back-to-back credit is not available from the issuing or advising banks.
- **Credit and insurance guarantees** (against default and political risks) provided by public or semipublic bodies are used to provide medium- and long-term credit to exporters/importers to promote exports and imports. The EX-IM Bank, the Private Export-Funding Corporation (PEFCO), and the Foreign Credit Insurance Association (FCIA) are examples of this type of credit help in the United States.

Documentary credits as instruments of financing encourage the growth of international trade, provide security in international commercial transactions, and serve as a means of receiving payments for goods and services exported. Financial management of both the multinational's risk and cash flows is greatly aided by these documentary credits.

INTERCOMPANY TRANSFERS TO/FROM/AMONG SUBSIDIARIES

Intercompany transfers between the parent and subsidiaries and among subsidiaries may also be used. Yet, this is more related to the overall strategies of establishing full-blown foreign operations, as discussed in Chapter 7. Nevertheless, the existence of an import-export network related to foreign subsidiaries can be viewed as beneficial for the multinational's domestic operations in cutting costs and enhancing revenues, as well as expanding foreign operations of the corporation. It allows the maximization of net gains from differences in costs, regulations, taxes, foreign exchange transfers, and so on, for the benefit of the domestic operations. (Transfer pricing and international repatriation and their use in this regard are discussed in Chapter 11.)

SUMMARY AND CONCLUSIONS

The multinational corporation can benefit directly or indirectly from import-export operations directly or indirectly related to its main business or new activities. There are many benefits from these operations both on the cost and revenue sides.

However, there are certain risks inherent here, and they should be managed by in-house expertise or external specialists—perhaps even agents. (These are discussed in terms of documents, transfers, and credit risks in this chapter; and in terms of government foreign exchange and blocked funds risks in Chapters 11 through 14.)

Focus for all of the import-export transactions, however, should ultimately be on the financial implications that increase the value of the corporation to its owners.

SELECTED REFERENCES

Abdullah, Fuad A., *Financial Management for the Multinational Firm*, Prentice-Hall, 1987, pp. 1–594, Chapter 7.

Chase Manhattan Bank, *Foreign Exchange: A Trade Perspective*, Second Edition, 1986, pp. 1–62.

Eiteman, David K., and Arthur I. Stonehill, with a contribution by Donald R. Lessard, *Multinational Business Finance*, Addison-Wesley, Fourth Edition, 1986, pp. 1–684, Chapter 14.

International Chamber of Commerce, *Guide to Documentary Credit Operations*, 1983 Revision, pp. 1–53.

Rodriguez, Rita M. and E. Eugene Carter, *International Financial Management*, Prentice-Hall, Third Edition, 1984, pp. 1–638, Chapter 8.

United States Department of Commerce, *Survey of Current Business* (monthly).

CHAPTER 6

Utilization of International Banks and Financial Markets for Domestic Operations

In addition to imports and exports to and from international markets for products and commodities, the international banking community and financial markets can be important adjuncts to any company's domestic operations. This is true for purely domestic businesses as well as for multinational corporations with extensive foreign operations and applies to both financing sources for capital requirements and investment opportunities for excess cash (or pension funds).

BANK LINES AND STANDBY CREDIT

Perhaps the most obvious benefits of the international financial markets are the lower rates and fees available to corporations for bank lines of credit. We have often seen the major international banks that do business in the United States quoting or accepting commitment fees that are approximately ten basis points or 40 percent lower than the standard fees that are charged by domestic U.S. banks of the same quality. For example, such quotes came from one of the big three banks in each of France, Germany, Switzerland, and the United Kingdom, and from one of the top banks in Japan, but from none of the top ten U.S. money center banks.

For letters of credit serving as both standby guarantees and payment mechanisms for trade imports, foreign banks operating in the United States are similarly more competitive on average. We have seen quotes of only 30–50 percent of those quoted by U.S. banks. Also, for trade requirements in some areas of the world, specific foreign banks can provide even more help. For example, British banks are more involved in many areas of the East and French banks are more involved in many areas of Africa. We saw the latter firsthand when CBS needed a letter of credit for importing materials into Nigeria.

EURO DEBT MARKETS

In a related area, the Euro capital markets developed a new facility in the 1980s that can serve the same purpose as a line of credit: Euronote issuance facilities called revolving underwriting facilities (RUFs). They have underwriting banks agree to purchase corporate notes at maximum interest rates when the market will not do so. Therefore, these facilities have often been used in lieu of bank lines of credit as backup facilities supporting U.S. commercial paper programs by helping to obtain higher ratings from Moody's or Standard and Poor's. The all-in costs are as low as ten basis points, such as the $200 million facility used by CBS in 1985. Again, major money center banks in Europe, Japan, Canada, and Australia have been more competitive as a group than U.S. banks; for example, the 12 banks in the CBS RUF were all from Europe, Japan, and Canada.

The note issuance facilities can be modified in form and purpose to provide a true alternative to the U.S. commercial programs. Euro commercial paper is a rapidly growing security market, although its total size is only $60 billion versus $365 billion in the U.S. market. Also, for U.S. corporate issuers (as opposed to foreign corporations or sovereign governments), only $15–20 billion has been issued. The basic problem has been the lack of better rates at most times, although some multinational corporations, such as Pepsico, have successfully used the markets to obtain favorable rates that often occur at some points in time.

For longer-term financing, the Euro debt markets can also provide advantages in both all-in interest costs and bond indenture terms, although this situation does vary over time. While in some cases a foreign subsidiary should be the borrowing entity, in most cases that is not required. Please keep in mind, this discussion involves financing for overall corporate needs, including purely domestic rather than international requirements; thus, this discussion is distinguished from the discussion of any favorable opportunities to finance foreign subsidiary requirements in Chapters 7, 8, and 9.

Perhaps CBS's 1987 $400 million Euro convertible issue can demonstrate both types of the potential benefits: lower all-in costs and more favorable indenture terms. The obvious starting point is analysis of pricing and terms, which are a function of interest rates and investor preferences in each market.

The Euro market demonstrated an interest rate advantage at some points over the prior three years (see the third quarters of 1984 and 1985 in Figure 6-1). Also, there were shorter windows in late 1984 and early 1986. Yet, in 1987, the general advantage appeared to be no longer present. Market saturation, fears about the dollar, fears of event risk—associated with U.S. corporate restructuring and increased leverage—were all advanced to us as possible explanations by many different investment bankers.

For CBS, the greater emphasis on name recognition and the reduced emphasis on ratings appeared also to have been favorable causal factors for lower costs in the Euro market at many points in time. CBS chose to make the prior two public debt offerings on the other side of the "Big Lake"—$100 million of Eurodollar notes and L 40 million of Eurosterling notes sold in December of 1984. Both issues were for straight debt, with maturities of eight and ten years, respectively. As in Table 6-1, CBS saved about 40 basis points and 70 basis points compared with dollar notes in the U.S. market. For the sterling issue, about 50 basis points were attributable to designation of the principal as a hedge of the company's sterling net assets, which is described in Chapter 13.

When the time came to issue convertible notes in 1987, there

FIGURE 6-1: *DOMESTIC VS. EURO MARKET FINANCING ADVANTAGE (1984 to 1987, 10-year maturity, AA rating)*

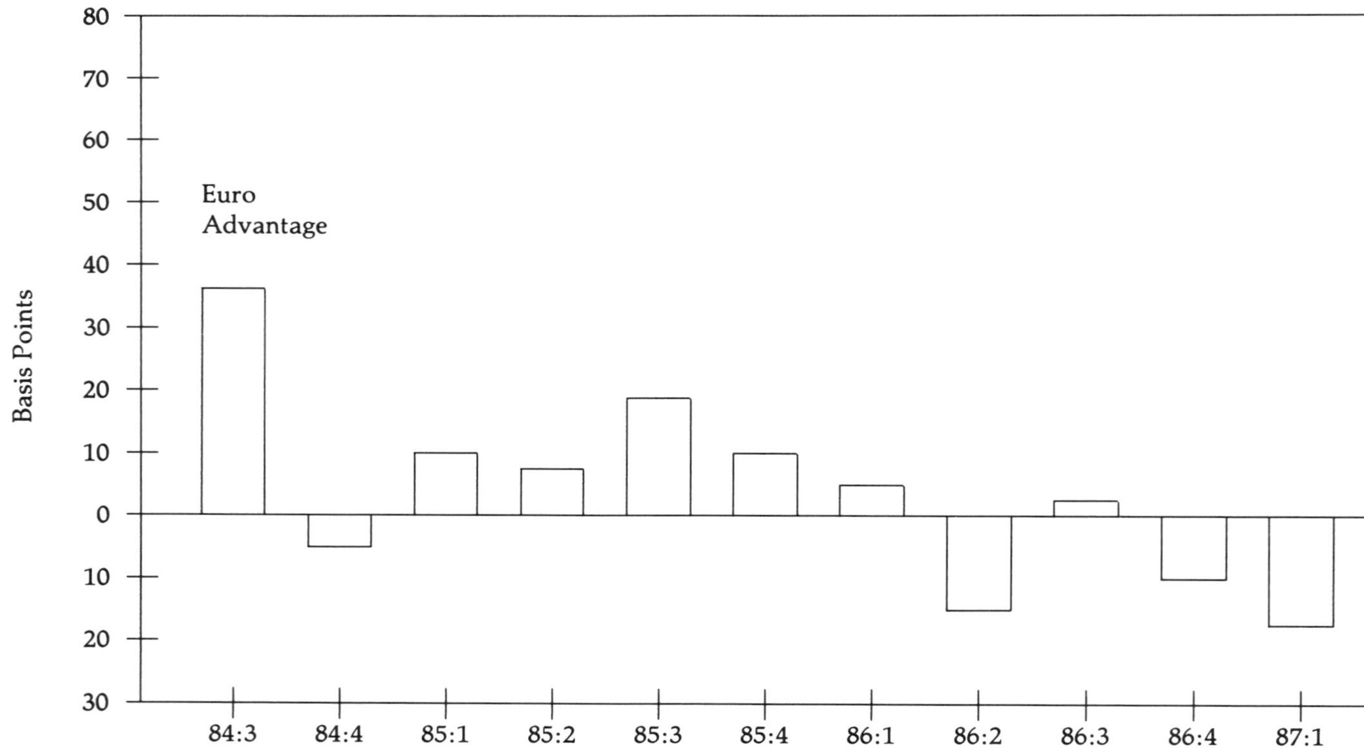

TABLE 6-1: *EURO MARKET ADVANTAGE FOR PRIOR CBS DEBT ISSUES*

	Annual Yield Dollar Costs[1]	
	Euro Issue	*U.S. Alternative*
$100 million, 8-year notes	11.5%	11.9%
L 40 million, 10-year notes	11.3[2]	12.0

[1]Semiannual yield basis
[2]Net components:

Sterling cost	10.9%
Forward cover	0.6
Designated hedges savings	(0.2)

were no general Euro rate advantages for the reasons discussed previously. Yet, investor appetite was strong for convertible bonds from high quality U.S. issuers. Few such quality issues had been available, and the convertibility feature helped diminish fears about corporate reorganization, higher leverage, and the weakening dollar. Again, for CBS, the benefits of name recognition versus ratings also appeared to be a strong plus.

The result was the all-in cost comparison shown in Table 6-2. The 5¼ percent all-in cost paid on the Euro convertible notes was

TABLE 6-2: *1987 CONVERTIBLE BOND ALL-IN COST ANALYSIS (annual yield basis)*

Term/Costs	*Euros*	*U.S. $*
Gross proceeds	$400,000,000	$400,000,000
Fees	(10,000,000)	(4,000,000)
Expenses	(100,000)	(100,000)
Net proceeds	$389,900,000	$395,000,000
Coupon	5%	5.25%
Annual interest	$20,000,000	—
Semiannual interest	—	$10,100,000
Repayment at maturity	$400,000,000	$400,000,000
All-in cost	5.25%	5.40%

about 15 basis points, or $600,000 less per year than what would have been paid if the convertible debt had been issued in the United States. The rate would have been 5.4 percent with the higher coupon rate and semiannual compounding in the U.S. market more than offsetting the lower U.S. issuance fees.

Apart from cost, there were also some other major benefits in using the Euro market: A bought deal, which guaranteed CBS a specific amount of proceeds on specific terms, was possible. However, in the United States the exact price could *not* have been fixed for 20 days or until the registration was approved by the Securities and Exchange Commission (SEC). This would have occurred after the deal was announced and the market reaction was felt, including the likely erosion of the common stock price for the equity dilution relative to a convertible issue. In fact, the stock price dropped by $4.00 immediately after the deal was announced.

Perhaps there is an analogy here to the selection of the Euro markets by most non-Japanese corporations for issuing yen debt versus entering the Japanese market itself. Pricing, syndication, approval, and so on, all appear to be quite uncertain for a much longer time after the initial debt decision is made in the domestic Japanese market versus the Euro market.

SPECIAL FINANCING OPPORTUNITIES

Apart from the potential competitive advantages in the international capital markets, some special opportunities such as those discussed in Chapter 9 are occasionally available. The following types of special financing are available to corporations with operations in certain countries:

- **Government-subsidized loans**
  - —Low-interest government loans
  - —Low-interest bank loans supported by the government
  - —Tax benefits
- **Creative financing**—such as:
  - —Sale/leaseback of films in the United Kingdom to get tax benefits

—Leasing-type structures in Japan to share the benefits of the high tax shield

However, in some cases, a multinational corporation with foreign operations may find itself with a worldwide incremental need for funds related to the domestic operations in its parent's home country. Then, the special opportunities cited above for the foreign subsidiaries may sometimes still be available to fulfill corporate requirements at favorable net costs of borrowing. This would merely be one example of utilizing the greater financial flexibility available to multinational corporations as a result of their involvement in and consideration of all of the world's marketplaces for both goods and capital.

CURRENCY/DEBT SWAPS

If a U.S.-based multinational corporation desires to finance a domestic operation with the lowest interest expense, another type of opportunity is available to it as a result of its foreign presence. If the corporation has net assets in countries with low local currency interest rates— as opposed to real or dollar-equivalent rates—debt denominated in dollars can be swapped for debt denominated in the local currency. This debt can then be designated under U.S. generally accepted accounting principles as a hedge of the foreign net assets.

As shown more fully in Chapter 13, this strategy allows the lower interest rates to flow through interest expense on the income statement. Yet, any expected unexpected offsetting of losses on the principal due to exchange rate fluctuations will be shown only in the special equity section of the balance sheet.

EQUITY ISSUES AND STOCK LISTING

Diversification of corporate ownership can provide three major benefits to most major corporations. First, when a particular segment of the investment community is adversely affected by some set of economic circumstances, the impact on the corporation's stock will be less. Second, if any increase in equity is desired through a new issuance of common stock, the potential size of the issuance and the resulting magnitude of the proceeds should be expanded if the investor market addressed is larger and more diversified. Third, if there is a challenge to the corporation's management control through a tender offer or a proxy fight, more widely held stock ownership can often help management more than the challenger.

These benefits can certainly be achieved through the international diversification of stock ownership as well as diversification of stock ownership within a given domestic market. For example, for a U.S.-based multinational corporation, stock appreciation could certainly have been greater in 1987–1988 for shares listed on the Tokyo Stock Exchange. Similarly, after the October "crash," the stock price decline could have been much less based upon the Tokyo index (Topix). Yet, on the Hong Kong, Portugal, and other exchanges, downward volatility was even greater.

In terms of the second benefit—the expanded purchasing capacity of new issues—we have seen some of the largest multinational firms utilize global issues in the U.S. and Euro markets in recent years. A notable example was the GMAC issue in 1987.

The third benefit of diversification may be even greater in the international arena. At times, non-U.S. shareholders seem to be more passive or supportive of incumbent management in takeover battles. This may be changing somewhat, as international takeover battles are becoming more commonplace.

However, despite these benefits, non-U.S. stock listings are not the standard practice for all U.S.-based multinational firms. The procedural requirements and related expenses have prevented all but a few American corporations from listing on the Tokyo exchange. While European exchange listings are more common, they are not universal; for example, CBS has not been listed on the major European exchanges for several years. Cost is again a negative factor.

We feel that another problem with international stock listing is psychological. It may be difficult to explain why your company's stock is dropping when other U.S. stocks are rising on the New York Stock Exchange. It may not be acceptable to members of the board or to shareholders that this is merely a result of disproportionate foreign ownership attributable to foreign listings and that in the long run arbitrage will keep prices in line on different exchanges in different countries.

EURO MONEY MARKET INVESTMENTS

In addition to all of the above financing and capitalization opportunities in the international markets, any corporation—even a domestic corporation—can often obtain higher rates of return on excess cash in these markets. At CBS, one of the primary bank deposits utilized has been Eurodollar time deposits. These deposits were often, but not always, placed with non-U.S. banks. Occasionally, nondollar Euro time deposits could be found that had such better returns that the net returns were higher even when the deposits were fully hedged with forward contracts back into dollars. (See Chapters 12 and 13 for exchange rate and hedging discussions.)

Recently, U.S. corporate pension funds have been getting more involved in international bond funds. They have greatly outperformed U.S. dollar bond funds in recent years, although this is mostly the effect of the weakening of the dollar's exchange rate since 1985. Yet, even on a fully hedged basis, some investment advisers and the trade press are now touting the benefits of international bond funds in reducing risk through diversification without reducing expected profit returns. (For the professional in the field, this is called shifting the "efficient frontier.")

Of course, pension funds have been even more active in international equity funds for a longer time. Their recent performance has been superior to that of U.S. stock returns. Also, a much lower percentage of the incremental return is attributable to recent exchange rate trends compared with bond funds. Looking forward, most investment advisers recommend some international equity participation for pension funds to improve the risk/return relationship (or shift the efficient frontier).

SUMMARY AND CONCLUSIONS

Domestic as well as multinational corporations can improve their financial performance by utilizing international banks and financial markets. They can do this by both seeking funds to invest in the business and investing excess funds generated by the business.

As a borrower, a corporation can use:

- **Bank facilities**
  —Bank lines of credit
    * Lower commitment fees and/or interest rates
  —Standby bank lines
    * Lower commitment fees
  —Euronote issuance facilities
    * Lower commitment fees to bank underwriters
    * CBS's $200 million 1985 RUF is an example with all non-U.S. bank underwriters

- **Debt capital markets**
  —Note issuance and Euro commercial paper programs
    * Lower interest rates at certain times
  —Eurobond markets
    * Lower interest rates at certain times
    * Better terms or covenants at certain times
    * Greater investor appetite for given issuers or types of bonds at certain times
    * CBS $400 million 1987 Euro convertible issue is an example of all three benefits

- **Special financing opportunities**
  —Government-subsidized loans
    * Low-interest loans from governments or local banks
    * Tax benefits to borrower
  —Creative financing in certain countries
    * U.K. and Japanese leases at times for tax benefits as examples

- **Foreign currency debt**
  - —New issues
    - * Fully hedged
    - * Greater investor appetite for market segment
  - —Currency debt swaps
    - * Fully hedged
    - * Still lower interest expense under U.S. generally accepted accounting principles if used as designated hedges of net assets

In addition to debt funds, corporations can obtain equity funds on a more favorable basis in the international markets. The following benefits may be available:

- **Better market conditions at certain times**
  - —Greater price appreciation
  - —Less price volatility from diversification
  - —Greater investor appetite for new global versus domestic issues
- **Less vulnerability in takeover battles**

On the other side of the balance sheet, corporations can improve returns on excess cash generated by utilizing international money markets. We have seen four major examples:

- **Eurodollar time deposits**
- **Nondollar Euro time deposits**
  - —Fully hedged against exchange rate risks (see Chapters 12 and 13 for exchange rate and hedging discussions)
- **International bond funds for pensions**
  - —Unhedged for currency potential
  - —Hedged for diversification and improved risk/return tradeoffs

- **International equity funds for pensions**
  —Unhedged since less sensitive to exchange rates
  —Improves risk/return trade-offs

SELECTED REFERENCES

Abdullah, Fuad A., *Financial Management for the Multinational Firm*, Prentice-Hall, 1987, Chapter 15.

Eiteman, David K. and Arthur I. Stonehill, with a contribution by Donald R. Lessard, *Multinational Business Finance*, Addison-Wesley, Fourth Edition, 1986, Chapter 12.

Rodriguez, Rita M. and E. Eugene Carter, *International Financial Management*, Prentice-Hall, Third Edition, 1984, Chapter 11.

PART III

FUNDING AND MANAGEMENT OF CASH AND CAPITAL FOR FOREIGN OPERATIONS

To obtain maximum benefits from expanded markets for their products and favorable sources for their supply of goods and materials, multinational corporations often create free-standing foreign operations. Usually, separate local subsidiaries are organized; and capital investments are made to establish these operations.

This section begins with a review of the issues and techniques employed to make the capital investment decision, discussed in Chapter 7. Then the sources and mix of debt and equity funding for both the capital investment and the working capital needs of the ongoing operation are discussed in Chapters 8 and 9. Once the operation is established, cash must be managed in an optimal manner through the collection of receivables, the disbursement of payables, the use of proper bank accounts, and the investment of cash in monetary instruments; and these items are covered in Chapter 10. Then cash must be transferred across national borders to be utilized within the worldwide operations and/or by the parent company, in addition to making payments to third parties in another country; and all such transfers are reviewed in Chapter 11.

CHAPTER 7

Evaluation of Capital Investments in Foreign Operations

When a corporation moves from having no prior international operation, having an export-import business, or having only a licensee arrangement to establishing full-fledged sales and manufacturing facilities in a given country, the benefits and costs of such direct investment must be carefully evaluated. As discussed in Chapter 5, the export operation expands sales markets for a company's products. A licensee arrangement represents even more direct involvement, with a local marketing and manufacturing organization becoming a representative of the company's product line. However, direct investment is the means of totally embarking on doing business in a foreign country.[1]

DIRECT FOREIGN INVESTMENT STRATEGY

There are usually one or two basic purposes for such expansionary investment. First, it is often easier from both control and public relations standpoints to supply a new foreign market with manufacturing or distribution from operations located within a foreign country. Also, it may be much more economical to insure local sources of intermediate and finished goods to avoid excessive freight costs. Second, foreign production may have a competitive advantage as a supply source for any of the corporation's worldwide markets, including the United States.[2] Having its own production allows a company to avoid the risks of importing the product and raw materials, as discussed in Chapter 5.

Of course, there are additional burdens and risks involved in establishing operations abroad. In addition to the investment required, the risk of doing business under foreign laws, procedures, and practices can often be a serious problem. Increased relations with a foreign populace—as both consumers and employees—may require a great deal of time and effort. If the U.S. firm has either a significant consumer brand advantage or technological superiority, it may overcome much of this hardship. Without such factors, foreign expansion beyond export-import operations may not always be practical or worthwhile.

Another characteristic of international expansion is the opportunity to obtain greater worldwide economies of scale.[3] While this is a definite element in making export and licensee decisions, the establishment of local facilities may yield little or no economies of scale from the additional revenue generated.

In short, while opportunities for foreign direct investment are significant and many firms have utilized this strategy quite effectively, careful evaluation will often lead to rejection of the expenditure proposals. We have seen many examples of losing operations of American firms in Latin America, Africa, and India. We have seen many attempts to compete with local operations in Western Europe and Canada fail. Today, China and Eastern Europe present wonderful market expansion opportunities, but profit from local operations is quite difficult for some businesses.

The incremental benefits in terms of cost savings and additional sales revenue must be specifically and realistically set out in the beginning. The effects on U.S. operations—that is, new export sales of finished and intermediate goods to the corporation's new foreign subsidiaries—must also be included. Also, the investment costs and risks of doing business in foreign lands must be considered fully. Finally, the alternatives of having export-import and licensee operations must be shown to be inferior before major direct investments are made abroad.

CORPORATE PHILOSOPHY TOWARD FOREIGN OPERATIONS

Once the benefits, costs, and risks of foreign capital investments are estimated, the standard domestic capital budgeting framework must be modified to make proper financial evaluations. First, however, the corporate philosophy toward the geography of its operations must be determined. Is this a true multinational corporation attempting to earn and reinvest money on a continuing basis in all countries around the world? Or is this a U.S. company seeking merely to add to domestic profits through selected transactions in foreign countries when opportunities arise?[4] For U.S. corporations as opposed to foreign-based parent organizations, the latter nationalistic approach may often be more representative of the views of shareholders, directors, and senior management.

As the degree of foreign investment and profits increases, U.S. companies begin to act more like true multinational corporations. Yet, in many specific procedures established—in the financial area, especially when new foreign investments are required—the nationalistic outlook may creep into the management approach and may influence decisions.

Another similar dichotomy is the parent company approach versus the project approach.[5] Are the local profits and investments important considerations, or should only the flows to and from the parent be taken into account?

In choosing the underlying basis for specific factors in the evaluation model discussed in the following section, we have attempted to combine the multinational and parent philosophies. The benefits and costs to the overall organization, as opposed to those of any given project, appear to be most relevant. After all, a corporation's management team in every country is employed by the overall organization and shareholders own an interest in that overall organization. However, this overall entity is not merely the holding company based in one country, such as a U.S. parent corporation, but the overall multinational corporate activity in all countries. The organization merely uses the U.S. parent as a central management, collection/disbursement, and reporting base.

KEY FACTORS IN THE EVALUATION PROCESS

To evaluate any capital investment, domestic or foreign, a discounted cash flow approach should be used. Maximization of the net present value of projects should be sought to implement the primary corporate goal of maximizing wealth for the shareholder.

For any cash flow evaluation model, some obvious key factors must be identified and calculated for foreign investments. Therefore, the starting point should be the precise definition of these key factors in a manner that will implement the corporate philosophy toward foreign operations.

There are four key factors in any disconnected cash flow model:[4]

- **Cash inflows** and outflows to be included
- **Tax rates** to use to obtain posttax cash flows
- **Inflation rates** to use for forecasting future cash flows
- **Cost of capital** to use as the hurdle rate or discount rate

However, for a foreign investment evaluation, the decision becomes much more complicated and somewhat controversial. Are the local foreign data, the U.S. data, or some combination of the two more relevant?

Designation of Cash Flows to Be Considered

A basic question that is most obviously affected by the corporate philosophy is determination of *which cash outflows and inflows should be attributed to a given capital investment and included in the discounted cash flow calculations.* Are cash outflows limited to funds coming from the parent company in the U.S., or are local uses of cash and increases in borrowing part of the investments? Are cash inflows limited to funds repatriated to the U.S., or should all cash generated by local foreign operations be treated as inflows to the multinational corporation?

Some corporate presentations would consider *only cash flows to and from the parent company* to be relevant. This *represents an ultimate example of the parent company philosophy as opposed to the project philosophy.* However, most approaches that we have seen in practice represent a *multinational perspective that considers both the parent and project cashflows. Any cash invested by or borrowed by either the parent or local foreign operations of the firm is treated as an investment made by the overall corporation. Any cash inflows to local foreign operations as well as to the parent are similarly treated as additions to the net cash flow.*

Without taking this multinational approach, an overly liberal view of local borrowing and an overly conservative view of income could result. The incurrence of local foreign debt to fund the majority of a project's needs would have no impact on the designated cash flow calculations, since no outflow from the U.S. would be required. Yet, for all consolidated subsidiaries, such debt would be reflected on the balance sheet. Thus, the incremental effect on the corporation's debt capacity would be understated. Similarly, no local earnings would be treated as a cash inflow until dividends or intercompany fee payments are made. For consolidated subsidiaries, this approach also understates earnings, at least in terms of the consolidated income statement.

One variation of the parent company method treats all cash outflows as investments, but then forecasts the maximum dividend payment being made to the parent from all cash inflows generated by the foreign operation.[5] This 100 percent dividend payout assumption can be defended as representing the logical use of funds, unless other projects require further investment. However, this approach *requires identification of a specific use of funds* for dividends. It also *bears no relationship to the concept of worldwide consolidated financial statements. Depreciation is also excluded from the cash flow,* although interest on depreciation cash funds may be treated as added income. Most important, there are many reasons that *a 100 percent dividend payout may not occur on a timely basis every year* for many subsidiaries.

For either a multinational corporate or a parent company approach as opposed to a project-based analysis, *incremental cash flows for operations in the United States and in other countries within the overall organization should also be considered. Fees earned and additional export profits must be added as inflows, and any costs or fixed or working capital investments required to sup-*

port these international transactions must be treated as outflows. We have even seen these nonlocal income streams represent the major portion of cash flows and present values for some businesses.

Blocked Funds Cash Flows. For operations that are deconsolidated because remittances of currency payments to the United States are blocked, perhaps both the multinational corporate and parent company approaches are both relevant.[4] In the long run, the cumulative cash flows should be the same, unless funds become blocked permanently; the latter is really an element of risk that is to be considered separately, as discussed below. Yet, the timing of all the cash flows can be very different.

Therefore, two net present value calculations should be prepared to provide the additional information needed for the decision maker. One set of cash flow projections would include all flows for the project, while the other would consider only flows to and from the U.S. parent company. We have seen this done in practice for projects whose risk of blocked funds is obvious—such as when first establishing new subsidiaries in less-developed countries.

Determination of Relevant Tax Rates

Determining the relevant tax rate under either the parent company or project philosophy would be easy. The U.S. or local country tax rates, respectively, would be the correct ones to use, except that foreign withholding taxes on dividends and U.S. tax credit regulations would be calculated specifically for each year's assumed dividend.[5] However, for a multinational corporate approach, what tax rate should be applied to all the cash inflows to the organization in all of the countries in which it operates, with dramatically different repatriation schedules?

We believe that for a U.S.-based parent corporation, the multinational approach should focus on the net effective U.S. tax rate as the ultimate effective rate that the organization will pay. If the funds are used by the overall organization via repatriation to the United States, the U.S. tax rate will obviously be paid.

If the funds are "repatriated" through other foreign subsidiaries and are used for investment in other foreign countries, the U.S. tax rates may be the best estimate of the average rates to be paid when funds are returned to the company for worldwide investment needs, rather than for local one-country use. While the time value of the deferred taxes will not be accounted for, if lower or higher rates are paid in foreign countries, we feel that they represent the least of the distortions among which we must choose.

Calculation of the net effective U.S. tax rate was simple for some companies when foreign tax rates were below U.S. rates and foreign tax credit regulations were less restricted. As a result of the full use of foreign tax credits, the U.S. statutory rate was a good estimate of the applicable marginal rate upon repatriation.

Of course, simplicity did not eliminate controversy. For example, one major acquisition represented a new product line expansion where the low average tax rates in "tax-haven" countries, which were source of about half of the profit derived, became a major issue. The low foreign tax rates were deemed temporary or fictitious benefits by some members of the corporate staff. On the other hand, the division sponsors could not understand why there was any problem in showing the high posttax income increase in the cash flows. In this, we feel the use of the U.S. tax rates by the corporate staff was warranted, though the upside of tax deferral for reinvestment of income should also have been considered.

Please note, however, that significant excess foreign tax credits now exist for most companies under the new U.S. tax law. In this case, when the higher local foreign taxes are applied to local income, additional U.S. tax credits will be generated upon repatriation of the earnings; however, these credits will merely add to the excess and will be of no value. In the few countries whose rates are still below U.S. rates, additional U.S. tax liabilities will be generated, but excess credits will always be available to offset them. Therefore, the result is that now the net effective U.S. tax rate will in most cases be the local foreign tax rate.

Identification of Relevant Inflation Levels

The next factor to be considered is inflation, which is really a combination of local inflation rates and foreign exchange rates. All cash flows must be denominated in one common currency for all time periods, regardless of the varying sources. For a U.S.-based parent corporation, the U.S. dollar is the obvious choice. All cash flows must also be denominated in current dollars rather than historical dollars because the present values calculation removes future inflation by including it as an element of the discount rate used.

These two requirements for the present value analysis appear to be consistent with all of the corporate philosophies—multinational versus national or parent versus project—because currency denomination and the time value of money are basic elements of any corporate financial analysis.

Two basic approaches can be used to project net inflation levels for dollar-equivalent cash flows. First, both local inflation rates and foreign exchange rates can be forecast. However, for a long-term major capital investment, this can be difficult to do. Second, a simpler approach can be used by removing inflation from all local cash flow projections and then reinflating the forecasts with the best estimate of U.S. inflation rates.

In the long-term life of a capital project, foreign exchange rate fluctuations should be caused by differences in inflation rates between one currency and another, which make one currency more or less valuable relative to the other. Thus, relative purchasing power should be maintained as higher inflation in one currency is offset by a lower future exchange rate for that currency. This concept is known as purchasing power parity.

Figure 7-1 shows an example of how purchasing power parity works.[4]

If purchasing power parity works in the long term, there is no need to forecast either exchange rates or local inflation rates. In fact, inflation differentials are the basis most widely used for forecasting long-term exchange rates. Forward market rates based on interest rate differentials can also certainly be used, but beyond one year, the forward market is not deep enough to be efficient. In any case, even forecasts of interest rate differentials are usually based on inflation differentials.

The latter concept, called interest rate parity and the Fisher Effect, is shown in Figure 7-2.[4] The concepts in Figure 7-2 are summarized and related to each other in Figure 7-3. The synthesis in

FIGURE 7-1: *PURCHASING POWER PARITY*

Assumptions	
Year 1	\$1.00 = LCY 1.00 1 widget costs \$1.00 1 widget costs LCY 1.00
Year 10	1 widget costs \$2.00 1 widget costs LCY 1.50 \$1.00 = LCY 0.75
Inflation	Inflation in \$ = 100% Inflation in LCY = 50%
Exchange rate	\$ devaluation = 25% LCY appreciation = 33%

Formulas/relationships

$$\text{New FX rate of \$/LCY} = \text{Initial rate of \$/LCY} \times \frac{1 + \$ \text{ inflation}}{1 + \text{LCY inflation}}$$

$$\frac{\$1.00/}{\text{LCY } 1.00} \times \frac{1.00 + 1.00}{1.00 + .50} = \frac{2.00}{1.50} = \frac{\$1.33/}{\text{LCY } 1.00}$$

therefore LCY worth 133% or 33% more

$$\text{New FX rate of LCY/\$} = \text{Initial rate of LCY/\$} \times \frac{1 + \text{LCY} \times \text{LCY inflation}}{1 + \$ \text{ inflation}}$$

$$\frac{\text{LCY } 1.00/}{\$1.00} \times \frac{1.00 + .50}{1.00 + 1.00} = \frac{\text{LCY } 0.75/}{1.00}$$

therefore \$ worth only 75% or 25% less

Figure 7-3 supports the use of purchasing power parity for the simpler approach in our capital evaluation model's handling of exchange rates and inflation rates. Only the U.S. inflation rate need be forecast, and all local currency data are translated into dollars at the current exchange rate.

FIGURE 7-2: *INTEREST RATE PARITY AND THE FISHER EFFECT*

(a) Interest Rate Components/Calculations	
$ Inflation	= 100%
LCY inflation	= 50%
Real returns	= 50%
$ interest	= (100% + $ inflation) (100% + real return) − 100%
LCY interest	= (100% + LCY inflation) (100% + real return) − 100%
$ interest	= (200% × 150%) − 100% = 200%
LCY interest	= (150% × 150%) − 100% = 125%
(b) Interest Rate Parity	
LCY premium % per arithmetic i.r.	= ($ i.r. − LCY i.r.)/(100% + LCY i.r.)
	= (200% − 125%)/(100% + 125%)
	= 75/225 = 33%
LCY premium % per forward market rate	= (100% + 200%)/(100% + 125%) − 100% = 33%
(c) Fisher Effect	
LCY premium %	= LCY appreciation % of initial exchange rate (from purchasing power parity example) = 33%
	= Expected increase in $ obtained per unit of LCY
$ discount %	= $ depreciation %
	= Expected decrease in LCY obtained per $

Calculation of Capital Costs and Required Returns

The most difficult factor to adjust for is the relevant cost of capital to be used as the required rate of return, which is then used as the discount rate in present value calculations. In reality, this involves potential adjustments for the cost of debt and for the cost of equity, which together comprise the cost of capital.

The differences between the costs of debt can be easily estimated by comparing local currency interest rates in dollar terms

FIGURE 7-3: *SYNTHESIS*

1. *Purchasing power parity*—Expected future exchange rate is function of inflation differential (Figure 7-1)
2. *Interest rate components/calculations*—Interest rate differential is function of inflation differential (Figure 7-2[a])
3. *Fisher Effect*—Expected future exchange rate is function of interest rate differential (Figure 7-2[c])
4. *Interest rate parity*—Forward rate is a function of interest rate differential (Figure 7-2[b])
5. *Synthesis*—Expected future exchange rate is function of forward rate (3 and 4), which is function of interest rate differential (3 and 4), which is function of inflation differential (1 and 2)

after accounting for forward market rates or inflation differentials. The following formula applies:

$$\text{\$ interest rate} = \left(1 + \text{LCY interest rate}\right) \div \left(1 + \text{forward rate premium}\right) - 1$$

The rates of most hard currencies should be similar to U.S. interest rates. For some Latin American countries, however, the dollar-equivalent rates could be high, based on risk, liquidity, or government policy factors.

Real interest rates in a given country can be relatively high or low due to differences in risk levels. The supply and demand for funds or specific central bank policies may also affect real interest rate levels. For the latter two items, the shift from negative real interest in Argentina—after foreign exchange rate adjustments in 1985 to a high positive real interest rate in 1986—appears to be a clear example. Brazil has also been cited as an example of high real interest rates in recent years. (These higher rates can be avoided by using nonlocal debt funding for the foreign subsidiary through intercompany loans, equity contributions, or retained earnings generated by local operations.) Yet, in most cases, the lower U.S. interest rates should be used for the cost-of-debt component of the capital costs, but should then be adjusted for the higher-risk premium that any local or U.S. bank would charge for financing the projects.

The interest rate risk differential has been used by some analysts to adjust the whole cost of capital. However, even if the risk is the only difference to be accounted for, its effect on the cost of equity is far greater and more variable. If there is a local stock market, the risk premium for equity versus debt can be estimated and compared with that in U.S. stock markets. That premium can then be added to the local interest rates expressed in dollar terms to determine the average cost of equity to be used. Specific adjustments for a company or business—that is, its own beta factors—can be applied to obtain its relevant cost of equity in a given country. Also, any additional risk of doing business as a nonresident-owned company must be subjectively evaluated. This risk has recently been raised as a major issue by the U.S. corporate community in Brazil.

Finally, the risk of currency becoming blocked can be accounted for by an additional risk adjustment. This may be more relevant for a nonresident company and, of course, cannot be included in local market risk premiums. Even a multinational outlook should incorporate some risk premium for currency usage limited to only one country where reinvestment needs may not grow adequately to use all funds generated. Nigeria is a good example of this; many companies wanting to expand in Africa have recently been hurt there. In fact, letters of credit are often required by exporters to Nigeria, and they are rarely available on a nonrecourse basis at interested banks.[4]

While the project philosophy would concentrate on local debt and equity rates, both the parent company and multinational approaches emphasize domestic U.S. capital costs and required returns. They are merely adjusted for the additional project risks, including the effect that presence in the foreign country has on the separate creditor and equity investor risks.

In any case, most of the companies that use such risk adjustments applied the adjustments to their standard hurdle rates. Many have even developed multiple standard rates for different countries, and nearly all require significantly higher returns for Latin America and other less-developed areas. For example, Brazil and Argentina have been prime investment candidates at some points in time for many American companies. Disappointing results there have led to a more cautious outlook today. Some previous investments have been liquidated and repatriated, and new investments usually require higher than normal incremental returns.[4]

Effects of Varying Foreign Capital Structures. We have seen some project sponsors on corporate staffs argue that the use of a lower return should be required for foreign capital expenditures whenever the foreign subsidiaries utilize more debt leverage in their local capital funds mix. International treasury managers often favor this higher debt level for many countries for one of four reasons: to reduce the risk of blocked funds, to facilitate a return of capital with fewer governmental restrictions than dividends have, to provide a hedge against local currency devaluation, or to avoid higher local real interest rates. (See Chapters 8 through 9 and 11 through 13.) Yet, apart from the riskiness of a given project or of doing business in a given country, these goals and requirements should not affect the relevant cost of capital or the required rate of return on an investment.

The overall capital structure of the worldwide organization is still the only issue that is relevant for such investment decisions. The consolidated financial statements for the organization will reflect such local debt levels unless the foreign subsidiary is deconsolidated; the latter represents a potential exception to the entire cash flow approach, as discussed above. Therefore, the only adjustments to the worldwide cost of capital that should be considered are risk adjustments for creditors and for equity investors that can alter the debt and equity component costs of the weighted average cost of capital. We feel that this approach is certainly consistent with the multinational corporate philosophy. It also represents the parent company approach when applied properly to the overall worldwide organization.

Effect of Foreign Government Subsidies. One exception should be made to the use of worldwide capital structure. If a multinational corporation can borrow money more cheaply in a given foreign country because of its presence there or the local capital spending that it incurs, this is a relevant benefit attributable to the local operation and project. (See the "Government and Subsidies" section of the discussion on financing foreign subsidiaries in Chapter 9.)

Apart from modifying the project's cash flow projections, as discussed in Chapter 9, one approach is to adjust for the difference in the posttax cost of debt. This will be the interest differential multiplied by (100 percent − tax rate). Then multiplying this by the worldwide percentage of debt in the total capital funds mix represents the actual adjustment to be made to the cost of capital.

Unlike differences in the local capital structure, the effect of subsidiaries will not be removed when the consolidated balance sheet is analyzed by rating agencies, investors, and so on. Instead, it represents a true change in the borrowing costs attributable to the local foreign operation. Thus, the benefit can and should directly aid in evaluation of the specific capital expenditures that generate it—by adjusting the hurdle rate for these expenditures.[6]

FOREIGN ACQUISITIONS

Acquisitions of foreign corporations and businesses represent another form of foreign capital investments that should be evaluated in a similar manner. In general, acquisitions should be evaluated as capital expenditures—at least in terms of the basic net present value calculations. Modifications are required in practice for many factors: operating synergies with the corporation's existing businesses, the greater significance of residual value, the nature of the sales and ancillary contracts required, the need for more due diligence, many legal and tax implications, and so on. Yet, the basic capital budgeting approach applies to acquisitions, even to the extent that the cash value of any stock exchanged should be included as a cash outflow for the initial investment.

Nevertheless, some additional considerations should be noted for foreign acquisitions as opposed to most foreign capital projects. Local management expertise may be more critical if an entire business is being acquired rather than only one operation being expanded. Negotiation with local management as sellers is often required and may represent a cultural communication gap. Local ownership may also be required, in part by government regulations or in part to insure success in a new business environment. Finally, the critical areas for any acquisition review and consummation process become much more complex. The three most common are the tax, accounting, and legal reviews. Obviously, local experts must be hired for each area.

SUMMARY AND CONCLUSIONS

A multinational corporation philosophy should be applied to the evaluation of capital investments in foreign subsidiaries. This approach is really the same as a parent company perspective, where the "parent company" is properly defined as all of the worldwide operations of the overall corporate organization as opposed to merely the U.S. holding company. This approach differs from either a project basis or a nationalistic outlook, which have been utilized by many corporations.

To sum up the approach for a multinational company, the four elements of our net present value calculations that are affected by international issues can be handled as follows:

- **Cash flow**—All cash flows from or to the company anywhere in the world should be included. Any locally incurred interest-bearing debt should also be treated as a cash outflow if it is consolidated on the worldwide financial books.
- **Tax rates**—The local tax rate is probably most likely to be applied to all worldwide pretax earnings of a U.S.-based corporation, given the likelihood of excess foreign tax credits.
- **Inflation rates**—U.S. inflation projections can be applied to all revenue and cost figures. Subsequently, neither local inflation rates nor future exchange rate fluctuations need be projected. Of course, adjustments to the general inflation forecasts can and should be made for specific factors such as price elasticity and margin erosion.
- **Required return**—A risk-adjusted, dollar-based cost of capital should be prepared for each type of business in each country to be used for the present value calculations. For the same risk levels, this should be the same as the corporation's general worldwide required return or cost of capital.

In practice, the only factor that should be difficult in the calculations is the required return adjustment. Calculation of real risk-adjusted costs of debt and equity can be very imprecise for a given country's capital markets, and adjustments for a firm's own product lines are probably even more subjective. Therefore, relatively standard hurdle rates may be the best solution; they can be estimated for many countries. Financial services are also available to categorize and quantify risk levels by country, and consultants can analyze projects.

We also recommend that internal rates of return, rather than present values, be calculated for foreign projects. Then, the decision makers can decide whether a given internal rate of return (IRR) is adequate for a given business in a given country. For example, a 20 percent return is probably inadequate for many Latin American and Third World countries, but is more than adequate for most businesses in Canada. For many investment decisions, obviously high-return and low-return projects will not require great precision in calculation of the hurdle rate.[4]

As with any capital budgeting decision, qualitative strategic factors must also be considered. There are two primary ones: First, what is the significance of the market opportunities that exist for the company's products and services outside of the United States? Is the revenue potential great enough, and can profitable returns be earned on the incremental investments in fixed and working capital that will be required? Second, does a U.S.-based parent bring enough to the party to operate effectively in a particular business in the foreign markets? For example, a purely labor-intensive, nontechnological service business may be run best by a locally owned company.

Perhaps a more interesting topic for discussion is the effect on overall corporate risk. Any multinational company will probably be involved in some countries whose political and economic risks exceed those of the United States. Yet, does the diversification of political and economic risk in general—through operations in several countries—reduce overall risk levels? Perhaps the real test should be the effect on the corporation's stock in the U.S. stock market for a multinational corporation compared with a company with purely U.S. operations.

If country diversification is a viable concept, opportunities can increase worldwide returns without increasing risk to the same degree. Portfolio theory suggests that if businesses are not highly positively correlated, investments in several risky projects or countries can be made without substantially increasing the overall corporation's portfolio risk. Since such risky projects and countries may offer the chance for very high returns, they could increase worldwide returns for the company without sacrificing overall safety.

However, the actual experience of many companies and banks in Latin America, Third World nations, and in South Africa does not generally support international diversification concepts. The stock market has also shown that such problems have a great impact on the value of corporate stock. For example, see the recent trends attributable to nonperforming loan exposures for any of our nation's largest banks.

While this entire discussion refers to many international purposes, nuances, and calculation adjustments that must be considered for foreign investments, the basic approach is consistent with capital budgeting techniques in general. The multinational philosophy merely calls for some modifications to the basic evaluation model so as to address specific quantitative and qualitative factors that vary from one country to another—just as they do from one domestic business to another or from one domestic market to another.

FOOTNOTES

1. Eiteman & Stonehill, *Multinational Business Finance*, Third Edition, Addison-Wesley, 1982, pp. 246–251.

2. Poinacheck, *Direct Foreign Investment in the U.S.*, Lexington Books, 1986, p. 15.

3. Eiteman & Stonehill, p. 256.

4. Krackov & Kaushik, *The Practical Financial Manager*, New York Institute of Finance, A Division of Simon & Schuster, 1988, Chapter 11.

5. Eiteman & Stonehill, Chapter 10.

6. Carter & Rodriguez, "International Budgeting," *International Finance Handbook*, Section 8.5, pp. 26–7.

SELECTED REFERENCES

Abdullah, Fuad A., *Financial Management for the Multinational Firm*, Prentice-Hall, 1987, Chapter 14.

Carter, E. Eugene, and Rita M. Rodriguez, "International Budgets," *International Finance Handbook.*

Eiteman, David K. and Arthur I. Stonehill, with a contribution by Donald R. Lessard, *Multinational Business Finance,* Addison-Wesley, Fourth Edition, 1986, Chapter 8.

Krackov, Lawrence M. and Surendra K. Kaushik, *The Practical Financial Manager,* New York Institute of Finance, A Division of Simon & Schuster, 1988, Chapter 11.

CHAPTER 8

Capitalization of Foreign Subsidiaries

Once it is decided to establish a full subsidiary operation in a foreign country to carry out marketing or manufacturing programs, the proper capital structure for that operation must be determined. The level of debt to be borrowed versus equity contributions to be made must be decided. The interest expense levels that must be borne by the operation will also be determined.

DESCRIPTION OF THE ISSUE

To some extent, this decision really concerns how much internal funds of the parent company or funds generated by the subsidiary should be used to finance the business—versus borrowing external funds from third parties. Any intercompany loans from the parent to the subsidiary, or vice versa, have basically the same effect on the multinational corporation's financial statements as an equity contribution or dividend. Yet, from the subsidiary's perspective, intercompany loans are also real loans to or from the subsidiary—just as if they were made to or from third parties, such as bank loans or bank deposits.

To some extent, the capital structure of a subsidiary is similar to that of the overall corporation. Yet, the levels of consolidated debt and equity are not the real issues; since high levels of either of these capital components at one subsidiary can be offset by low levels at another subsidiary or at the parent company. Therefore, several other factors critical for running the subsidiary apart from the overall corporation must be considered, apart from consolidated debt/equity ratios.

Factors to Consider

At least four factors affect the subsidiary capital structure decision that are different for the overall capital structure of the consolidated corporation:

- **Future cash movements** to and from the subsidiary are a primary concern. Unlike funds in most domestic subsidiaries of parent companies, the multinational corporation's funds in many subsidiaries cannot be moved, whenever desired, to or from the parent company for use in the business wherever needed. A capital structure that maximizes the flexibility of such future movements may, therefore, be greatly preferable to one that could lock funds up.
- **Local management incentives** are obviously affected by the debt and equity levels of their subsidiary. The most direct effect is the level of confidence that management has in the security of the balance sheet. Is their subsidiary corporation financially sound by the local standards of other competing and noncompeting companies? More indirectly, the income effect of more or less interest is a major psychological factor. In fact, some local managers say that they cannot effectively operate when interest blocks their chances of showing an adequate profit. Finally and perhaps more important, pricing, working capital, and investment decisions are all affected by the amounts of interest shown on the income statement and by the profitability ratios that measure local management performance, such as returns on equity.
- **Creditor perceptions** of local suppliers and banks are important for the subsidiary's ability to operate in the local foreign environment. The overall multinational corporation's financial position may not be relevant, especially if no guarantees are pro-

vided to support subsidiary liabilities and if no worldwide relationship exists between the overall corporation and the creditors involved.

- **Government perceptions** are similarly critical for the subsidiary to operate, and foreign governments prefer adequate equity for companies operating within their borders.

Also, at least two factors are generally not included in local subsidiary decisions:

- **Local interest rates** relative to the parent company's or worldwide borrowing rates are not relevant in most cases. First, the rates, adjusted for differences in exchange rate forecasts, are usually the same. Second, even if a given country has better borrowing opportunities, such loans can be obtained for the multinational corporation through any one of a number of legal entities, including the parent company's direct borrowing. The decision at hand concerns the level of debt that should be placed on a local subsidiary's books, as opposed to where it should be borrowed.
- **Lowest cost of capital** is usually the benchmark by which the overall corporation's optimal capital structure is measured. Yet, this is not the case for a subsidiary, as previously discussed. How the overall level of debt should be allocated among different subsidiaries—not how high the overall level should be—is the decision at hand.

VARIOUS APPROACHES IN THEORY AND PRACTICE

To obtain one or more of the above goals, at least four approaches to setting capital structures for foreign subsidiaries have been used or seriously considered by major multinational corporations:

- **The autonomous approach** designates the subsidiary capital structure as if the subsidiary were an independent company.

Neither the parent nor other affiliates within the multinational corporation are considered. Naturally, this approach addresses the local management psychology, creditor perceptions, and government perceptions.

- **Minimum equity funding** concentrates on the goal of cash-movement flexibility. Cash generated by the business can reduce capital invested in the business by retiring local foreign debt. Intercompany debt can also be used for this purpose, but only when intercompany debt repayments are completely unrestricted, which is often not the case. Dividends to the parent company can also be used to repatriate cash as well as other intercompany payments discussed in Chapter 11, but these are all more restricted by government regulations to a greater or lesser extent. In any case, the existence of a minimum equity level that is consistent with minimum government and creditor requirements will allow the maximum debt to be employed for the maximum flexibility in eliminating excess cash—by repaying local or intercompany debt, thus reducing the investment in the business.
- **Operating decision to provide working capital funding** with debt and fixed asset funding with equity focus on a portion of the management incentives. This approach separates investment decisions into daily local management decisions and longer-term corporate decisions. Desirable or prudent increases in working capital should produce immediate profits in excess of the interest expense on debt. However, increases in fixed assets may have a much longer pay-out. Local management must evaluate working capital levels daily, whereas fixed asset levels are more of a longer-term strategic decision for corporate planners.
- **Profitability targets,** such as a minimum return on equity level, can be set to limit the amount of debt or equity that can be used. In practice, these targets may be more of a rationalization by corporate management to be presented to local management to show that adequate return levels can be achieved, despite payment of interest on debt. (In fact, higher debt and lower equity will often improve the return as long as a minimum return on assets is attained in excess of interest rates.)

The effect of these various approaches can be quite significant in determination of the level of debt. The different debt/capital ratios for each approach are shown in Table 8-1.[1]

TABLE 8-1: *DEBT/CAPITAL RATIOS FOR VARIOUS APPROACHES*

Assumptions	
Local/competitor debt/capital ratios	= 40%
Legal minimum equity level	= 20% total assets
Total assets	= $100, with $50 fixed and $50 current
Trade payables	= $25
Profit before interest after taxes	= $10
Posttax interest	= 5%
Return on earnings target	= 20%

	Debt	*Equity*	*Debt/Capital Ratio*
Capital structure			
Autonomous	$30	$45	40%
Debt = 40% × $75*			
Minimum equity	55	20	73
Equity = 20% × $100			
Operating decision	25	50	33
Equity = $50			
Return on earnings target	33	42	44
Return on earnings = ($10 − $1.65)/$42			

*Capital = total assets less interest-free liabilities.

CAPITALIZATION IN VARYING REAL INTEREST COUNTRIES

As previously stated, interest rates in most countries are similar to each other once adjusted for foreign exchange rate forecasts. For the major currencies, these forecasts are represented by forward market rates. The forward market can also be used to combine forward contracts with any borrowing strategy to lock in interest rates that are similar to the real rates in most major money centers, such as New York.

In some countries, however, where capital movement restrictions apply and a forward market for foreign exchange is unavailable, interest rates in dollar terms can often be very high or very low. This is often the case in hyperinflationary countries such as Brazil, Argentina, and Mexico. One school of thought holds that such differences are short term. Thus, they should not have an impact on any longer-term financial strategies such as the proper local foreign capital structure. Indeed, it is often impossible to obtain long-term debt in these capital and banking markets.

If the rare exception is found in which a government policy or risk factor reduces or increases real long-term interest rates, special strategies may be called for. If a government policy is affecting lower or higher real interest rates—such as a lower peso to support Mexican exports or a higher cruzado to reduce Brazilian inflation—greater or lesser debt should be included accordingly in the local capital mix. Yet sometimes, in lower-rate countries, the parent can still accomplish this by borrowing locally and injecting the funds as an equity contribution. Analogously, sometimes, in high-rate countries, intercompany loans from the parent at lower dollar-equivalent interest rates could be used to reduce external borrowing costs while leaving the subsidiary with the desired amount of debt. In other words, the goal is to separate the decision about the proper capital structure for the operation from the effects of high- or low-interest funds.

When high interest rates are a function of higher local risks, this would call for some special strategies. Such risks are usually related to the potential expropriation of assets or the blockage of funds for multinational corporations. If this risk element is present, the special financing considerations discussed in Chapter 9 should be evaluated.

RELATIONSHIP OF SUBSIDIARY CAPITALIZATION TO OVERALL CORPORATE CAPITAL STRUCTURE

While the local capital structure of a foreign subsidiary is separate from the overall capital structure of the multinational corporation, there are obviously some areas of relationship.[2] First, if other portions of the corporation are highly leveraged with debt and more debt is deemed desirable, borrowing by a moderately leveraged subsidiary may be more practical than borrowing by the parent. Although the parent could make intercompany loans or equity contributions to the subsidiary, borrowing may still be done more easily at the subsidiary level.

Second, the other extreme can also exist. Highly leveraged corporations may have subsidiaries incapable of obtaining credit in local markets, where such high debt levels may not be understood. The parent corporation's domestic money markets may be more receptive to such capital structures—in general or for corporations with a good local reputation.

Third, the local capital structure required may be one of low debt, even if this may increase the possibility of a buildup of local foreign cash that cannot be or will not be repatriated, as discussed in Chapters 11 and 12. In some cases, the corporation will then merely borrow more at the parent level or at other subsidiaries. In other cases, the corporation's capital structure at the parent company level or in the other subsidiaries will be viewed separately by the creditors and capital markets that the corporation utilizes. Then a higher level of debt in such places will not be feasible, and the overall capital structure will become underleveraged on a consolidated basis. However, this will not be a problem for unconsolidated and deconsolidated subsidiaries.

CAPITALIZATION FOR VARYING TYPES OF BUSINESS

Foreign subsidiaries and businesses in general should be more highly leveraged when higher levels of cash and liquidity are generated compared with earnings levels. Therefore, a good cash flow business, or one with a highly reserved balance sheet may allow the corporation to utilize more debt than equity funding.[2] However, capital-intensive business may require more equity (although for a subsidiary, the availability of future intercompany funding in an emergency somewhat mitigates this requirement).

CAPITALIZATION AND MANAGEMENT PERFORMANCE

The most obvious relationship of the local subsidiary capital structure to capital expenditures is under the generally accepted matched funding concept. Long-term investments in property, plant, and equipment—and even the permanent levels of net working capital or current assets less interest-free liabilities—should be funded with long-term financing. Funding of the assets required merely to remain in business will then be less vulnerable to refunding after changes in future interest rates.

If long-term debt is not available in the local marketplace, the corporation has the choice of making an equity contribution or an intercompany loan to the subsidiary from the parent or another subsidiary to fund long-term asset requirements. The parent or other subsidiary can finance the funds to be loaned with external debt, external stock, or internal retained earnings. However, flexibility in determining the original foreign subsidiary's capital structure has been eliminated.

An even more important and complex decision is the relationship of the local foreign capital structures available to the multinational corporation to the required return which is used to evaluate foreign capital spending decisions. Generally, however, as discussed in Chapter 7, the only relevant cost of capital for such investment decisions is that of the corporation's consolidated capitalization. Also, the only major exceptions to this approach are the evaluation of different risk levels to be used for doing business in a given country and the presence of government-subsidized debt. In investment decisions, therefore, the specific capital structure used for a given foreign subsidiary should have little effect on the evaluation process.

Of course, the risk of blocked funds is a separate subject that is critical in the evaluation of investments. This is discussed in Chapters 7 and 12.

In terms of shorter-term decisions for managing working capital, several factors favor a highly leveraged approach to financing this portion of the balance sheet. The use of debt financing in general will limit the buildup of excess cash, which is one of the reasons that working capital levels become too high. If debt is used to fund the temporary fluctuations or incremental increases in working capital that are related to seasonal business volume fluctuations or business expansion, local management will have every incentive to control receivables and inventory levels tightly. This will insure that profits from incremental sales more than cover the incremental interest cost (though this is admittedly below the required return on capital for the incremental investment).

DIVIDENDS FROM FOREIGN SUBSIDIARIES

The amount of dividends that should be remitted from a foreign subsidiary, as discussed in Chapter 11, is obviously one of the ongoing financial decisions that determines the capital structure for that subsidiary. Apart from future capital spending requirements, the levels of retained earnings, and thus equity, that exist at the subsidiary will be a function of the dividends removed from the earnings generated by the business. Therefore, a dividend remittance policy should be set for each foreign subsidiary in line with the capital structure targets established for each subsidiary by the multinational corporation.

The following approach will demonstrate how these goals can be implemented in practice:[1]

- **Calculate actual equity level**—Stock, plus retained earnings, plus interest-free intercompany liabilities.
- **Define target equity level**—Based on the target capital structure.
- **Calculate excess or deficiency of equity**—Subtract the target equity from the subsidiary's actual equity level.
- **Designate dividends to be paid or equity to be contributed**—The goal is to eliminate any excess or deficiency of equity. For the lattter, we may merely use a deferral of a dividend until an excess equity level is obtained for dividends, rather than an equity contribution. For desired dividend payments, however, if there is a lack of legal remittance capacity, the legal dividends should be declared and paid to the parent company or any other affiliate that is the immediate parent of the subsidiary. Then, any fur-

ther excess equity in (3) could become an "internal" dividend to a corporate division, whose funds are shown on special internal financial statements to be prepared locally or by the parent.

SUMMARY AND CONCLUSIONS

The multinational corporation's designation of the desired capital structure of a foreign subsidiary is basically distinct from the decision that establishes its overall consolidated capitalization targets. Four factors should be considered in determining the appropriate local foreign capital structure:

- **Future cash levels** and cross-border movements
- **Management incentives** for local foreign managers
- **Creditor** perceptions and requirements
- **Foreign government** perceptions and requirements

Paradoxically, however, the level of local interest rates in different countries is generally not a factor, since most foreign interest rates and U.S. dollar interest rates are usually the same on a foreign exchange-adjusted basis. Similarly, the key overall capitalization goal for the lowest cost of capital should usually not be considered relevant for the allocation of the overall debt/equity component percentages to individual foreign subsidiaries.

Incorporating one or more of the four relevant factors leads to at least four approaches that we have seen used or seriously considered in practice:

- **Autonomous approach**—Treating each subsidiary as a standalone foreign company.
- **Minimum equity**—Maintaining maximum local debt and minimum equity, either contributed by the multinational corporation or retained from local earnings.
- **Operating decision—funding working capital**—With debt, but funding all fixed assets with equity.
- **Profitability targets**—Ensuring adequate returns on equity for which local management is responsible (more of a rationaliza-

tion for discussion with local managers than a target-setting approach).

In terms of debt percentage levels, the minimum equity approach should usually result in the highest debt/capital level and the operating decision approach should usually result in the lowest level.

Other factors that occasionally affect foreign subsidiary capital structure decisions are:

- **Continuance of high real interest** levels in some hyperinflationary countries at some points in time
- **Debt level constraints or opportunities** in light of the overall level of debt or the levels in other portions of the multinational corporation

Finally, the specific decision on foreign subsidiary capital structures should incorporate the following operating and management issues and functions:

- **Type of business** involved at the subsidiary
- **Capital spending evaluation process** (though this should usually be treated as separate and unrelated to the local capital structure)
- **Working capital management**
- **Management performance incentives**

In addition, foreign dividend remittances, as discussed in Chapter 11, should be directly related to the local capital structure targets established. In other words, the amount of dividends should leave the desired amount of equity in the subsidiary—neither more nor less.

FOOTNOTES

1. Krackov and Kaushik, *The Practical Financial Manager*, New York Institute of Finance, A Division of Simon & Schuster, 1988, Chapter 22.

2. Krackov, Financing Foreign Operations of Multinational Corporations, *Handbook of International Corporate Finance*, Allen & Unwin, 1989.

SELECTED REFERENCES

Abdullah, Fuad A., *Financial Management for the Multinational Firm*, Prentice-Hall, 1987, Chapter 10.

Eiteman, David K. and Arthur I. Stonehill, with a contribution by Donald R. Lessard, *Multinational Business Finance*, Addison-Wesley, Fourth Edition, 1986, Chapter 12.

Krackov, Lawrence M., "Financing Foreign Operations of Multinational Corporations," *Handbook of International Corporate Finance*, Allen & Unwin, 1989.

Krackov, Lawrence M. and Surendra K. Kaushik, *The Practical Financial Manager*, New York Institute of Finance, A Division of Simon & Schuster, 1988, Chapter 22.

Rodriguez, Rita M. and E. Eugene Carter, *International Financial Management*, Prentice-Hall, Third Edition, 1984, Chapter 9.

CHAPTER 9

Financing of Foreign Subsidiaries

Once the multinational corporation establishes capital structure targets for a foreign subsidiary, the next task is to arrange for specific funds to finance the local operating and capital requirements.

INTERNAL FUNDING FROM THE SUBSIDIARY CASH FLOW

The starting place for any funding decision is obviously to utilize any excess cash left from cash flow generated by the business. For a given subsidiary, this will be a function of the equity determined by the local capital structure of the subsidiary as well as the cash generation level of the business.

Once the target equity level is designated and dividends are paid accordingly, all excess cash should be invested in the business to the greatest extent possible. If excess cash is allowed to remain, the return on its investment in a money market will be only about one-third of the required return. Thus, for any financing needs, such cash should be utilized first.

In fact, if financing needs do not exist, additional dividend remittances should be considered, as discussed in Chapter 11.

These will allow the repatriated funds to be available for investment in other countries or for debt retirement and stock repurchases by the parent.

DETERMINING CASH LEVELS IN DIFFERENT COUNTRIES

Some excess cash can build up in a given country's subsidiary operations, despite any multinational corporate goal or policy. Management psychology and politics can require special dispensation to keep a given local manager properly motivated or content. Legal restrictions in some countries can prevent implementation of the desired dividend remittances.

As discussed in Chapter 11, intercompany fees can circumvent some of these problems, but certainly not in all cases. In some countries, intercompany loans from the subsidiary to the parent or to another subsidiary can also alleviate both legal and management psychology problems. However, intercompany loans are restricted in most countries, at least to some extent (see Chapter 11.) U.S. parent companies also have the added concern of a potential deemed-dividend tax problem if such loans are used continuously beyond one year.

In extreme situations, all dividends and external payments may even be totally blocked from a given country. This is a related but separate issue that is discussed in Chapter 12. Many preventive measures and remedial strategies against inadequate repatriation of funds are discussed in Chapters 12 and 14. When these fail to be completely successful, excess cash will probably build up and be available to fund primarily local financing requirements.

In terms of financing needs, the lack of availability of cash may be a more critical problem. Internal funds are not available whenever the following situations occur:

- **Operations are starting up.**
- **Operations are expanding.**
  —Capital spending is required.
  —Working capital is growing.

- **Company operates at a loss.**
  —Profitability has not yet reached a level adequate to fund local needs.
- **Capital infusion from parent is prohibited.**
  —Equity investment restrictions exist.
  —Intercompany loan restrictions exist.
- **Parental contributions are risky.**
  —Blocked funds are a potential problem.
  —Foreign exchange devaluation is a problem.

Thus, even when internal funding may be desirable based on the optimal capital structure, cash may not be available from a practical perspective. In this case, the external sources outlined below must be used. However, as profits are generated or any other circumstances change, external borrowing can probably be replaced with internal funds. Therefore, external funding should be selected with that possibility in mind. The following are some factors to consider when making financing decisions so as to insure this future refinancing flexibility:

- **Preference for debt** in local funding versus local stock sales
- **Preference for short-term maturities** for local loans or for allowance of prepayment without penalties

INTERCOMPANY LOANS AND TRADE CREDIT

When the target capital structure for the subsidiary calls for local interest-bearing debt to be used for a given foreign subsidiary's financing needs, external debt funds should normally be sought. However, such funds are sometimes unavailable. Also, at times their terms appear uneconomical, such as when the dollar-equivalent interest rates are much higher than interest rates in the United States. In such cases, intercompany loans can be used.

From the subsidiary's perspective, such intercompany loans appear to be interest-bearing debt. From the parent company's perspective, intercompany loans are a hybrid. As long as the balance is outstanding, there is an equity risk of blocked funds. There is also the elimination of debt on the consolidated books, which leaves the ultimate funding classification to be that source of funds used by the parent to provide the funds sent to the subsidiary. This source can be any type of debt or equity of the parent, as if the parent were funding an equity contribution to the subsidiary.

It should be noted that the remittance of intercompany loan repayments and interest may be somewhat easier than that of dividends. Thus, the risk of building excess cash may be somewhat less, analogous to that of local debt.

When an interest-free financing of the subsidiary is the desired strategy but equity contributions are considered inappropriate, intercompany trade credit can merely be extended beyond the normal term. In this way, all of the advantages of an intercompany loan can be created without interest being charged. But if the term goes beyond 180 days, a U.S. parent may need to charge interest to avoid tax problems.

Finally, if there are corporate bank accounts or bank accounts of other subsidiaries in the same country, intercompany loan funding can be created automatically through an overdraft in the bank account of the subsidiary that requires financing. The intercompany loan effects and the elimination of the loan payable and receivable upon consolidation in the bank pool are shown in the discussion of repatriation in Chapter 11. In other words, with intercompany loans, intercompany trade credit, and bank pools, loan financing for one subsidiary can be the same as repatriation of funds from the other subsidiary. All these mechanisms can be used to make the best use of the cash, wherever located, for the benefit of the multinational corporation.

EXTERNAL SOURCES OF DEBT

For most companies, local bank loans and lines of credit are the most common and easiest to use of all external sources of financing. The advantage of lines of credit—whether automatically approved loans or merely allowed overdrafts in local bank accounts—is their flexibility to fit exactly both temporary and seasonal needs. This can be especially useful for subsidiaries whose debt interest rates or debt service requirements are considered an income statement or cash flow burden—such as those in hyperinflationary countries with high local interest (e.g., Brazil).

When the needs are for a longer time frame, however, uncertainty is a major concern in terms of both interest rate trends and the availability of refinancing sources. For these longer-term needs, interim loans with fixed maturity dates can be an operating necessity allowing the local operation to implement its normal business strategies without undue financial fears.

In many countries, similar financing can be arranged on even more favorable terms from two other sources:

- **Other multinational corporate subsidiaries**—Especially in hyperinflationary countries where cash-rich businesses have difficulty in obtaining adequate positive real interest returns at banks.
- **Local capital markets**—Commercial paper and similar local paper or Euronotes, which can be used to obtain nearly the same rate and flexibility benefits as commercial paper in the United States.

Longer-term debt funds may also be available in some capital markets for some large foreign subsidiaries. If such subsidiaries have their own name recognition in the marketplace, they may borrow in these markets as efficiently as or more efficiently than the parent company could. The foreign subsidiaries may even be capable of issuing notes and bonds in their local markets or even in the Euro markets, as their U.S. parent could in the United States.[1]

Local capital markets can be used as an alternative to the parent company's borrowing in its own saturated capital markets. More favorable terms may be available in local markets—such as lower interest rates, easier loan covenants, or more favorable structures—and local borrowing can often be done more easily by a locally known subsidiary. In any case, one of two other benefits can be obtained by having the subsidiary borrow its own debt in the local capital market on behalf of the corporation: either the necessity of an equity contribution to the subsidiary will be avoided or foreign currency debt exposure for the subsidiary, or an intercompany loan, which would necessitate buying a long-term forward foreign exchange contract, will be avoided. See the discussion on managing foreign exchange rate risks in Chapters 12 and 13.

In some cases, local debt is simply not available for companies on a stand-alone basis. This often occurs in high-risk countries or in local subsidiaries without a proven record or sound balance sheet. One of two approaches could be taken.

First, the multinational corporation could give parental guarantees to the local creditor or the creditor's parent. For a consolidated subsidiary, all of the attributes of local borrowing would be maintained except for the transfer of risk. (Even without a guarantee, the corporation would usually voluntarily support repayment of local borrowing if the local debt was arranged by the corporate staff.) For an unconsolidated subsidiary, however, the guarantee would be shown in the footnotes to the consolidated corporate balance sheet, which would add to the consolidated debt ratios for most credit analyses and bond ratings.

Second, matched funding could be provided by the parent outside of the local country. This is a very good approach for everyone concerned so long as the multinational parent has excess cash for the funding and a preference for external financing, rather than as an intercompany loan (or restrictions prevent use of the excess cash for an intercompany loan to the local subsidiary). However, if there is no excess cash, the corporation's overall consolidated debt and capital levels increase due to external borrowing by both the parent and the subsidiary. The cost of this increase can be the difference between the corporation's required return on capital of 25–30 percent and the lower money market rate that it earns on the matched-fund loan to the other party. (See the analogous discussion for repatriation in Chapter 11.)

ASSET-RELATED DEBT

Collateralized financing can be a good way for a financially troubled foreign subsidiary to establish its own credit.[1]

Real estate mortgages may be used for the local plant or office buildings as easily as in the United States. This is especially true if financing proceeds are being directly used to build or buy such real estate.

Similarly, receivables and inventory financing are available in many countries, as they are in the United States. Factoring of receivables, with or without recourse to the subsidiary by the creditor, helps alleviate the creditor's risks. This is even truer when the creditor provides full-service factoring, and thereby has the credit analysis collection capability itself. Inventory floor-plan financing also alleviates some risk, at least when the goods are relatively fungible and resalable, such as automobiles.

Since leasing also leaves specific assets in "the hands of the creditor" (the lessor), reasonable stand-alone financing may be obtained in this manner. Usually, true implicit interest rates of leasing will be higher than those of good bank loans—just as in the United States—but the latter may be unavailable to a financially troubled subsidiary. The implicit interest rate can be calculated as shown in Table 9-1, where the posttax rate is the incremental internal rate of return of 7 percent and the pretax interest rate is 14 percent.[2]

Off-balance-sheet treatment may be available for certain forms of asset-based borrowing. Factoring of receivables without recourse may be treated as a sale of the receivables. Leasing or a sale/leaseback may also leave the fixed asset, whether real estate or equipment, on the lessor's balance sheet and off the subsidiary's balance sheet. If the financial ratios—such as the return on capital or the debt/capital ratio—are key factors, this possibility may be enough of a benefit to justify the higher interest rate of leasing or factoring. If so, a careful review with the public accountant must be made as to the allowance of the off-balance-sheet treatment, in general, and as to any restructuring of the factoring or lease agreements that would be required.

GOVERNMENT SUBSIDIES

Perhaps the best form of foreign debt funds for subsidiary operations is provided or supported by local government. For many economic reasons, such incentives are given for expansion of local production, assistance of the export business, and even importation of critical technological products.

TABLE 9-1: *BUY/LEASE ANALYSIS (inflows/outflows)*

	Year					
	0	*1*	*2*	*3*	*4*	*5*
Purchase						
Purchase price	$1,349					
Sales tax @ 4⅝%	62					
Total purchase price	$1,411					
Service		$49	$49	$49	$49	$49
Property tax		3	3	2	2	2
Depreciation		337	289	242	193	144
Total ord. expense		$389	$341	$293	$244	$195
Proceeds from sale						$(270)
Net book value						144
Gain on sale						$(126)
Ordinary inc. taxes	$(31)	$(195)	$(170)	$(147)	$(122)	$(98)
Capital gains taxes						31
Total income taxes	$(31)	$(195)	$(170)	$(147)	$(122)	$(67)
Investment tax credit	$0					
Total costs	$1,380	$195	$170	$147	$122	$4
Noncash items[1]	—	337	288	242	193	289
Net cash cost—purch.	$1,380	$(142)	$(118)	$(95)	$(71)	$(285)
Lease						
Rent		$377	$377	$377	$377	$377
Sales tax @ 4⅝%		18	18	18	18	18
Property taxes		3	3	3	3	3
Total ord. expenses		$398	$398	$398	$398	$398
Inc. taxes @ 50%		$(199)	$(199)	$(199)	$(199)	$(199)
Net cash costs—lease		$199	$199	$199	$199	$199
Incremental calculations						
Net cash flows	$1,380	$(341)	$(317)	$(294)	$(270)	$(484)

[1]Depreciation and book value upon disposition.

The incentives usually take one of three forms:

- **Low-interest government loans**—Direct from the government
- **Low-interest bank loans**—With benefits or requirements given to the banks by the government
- **Tax benefits to the borrower**

If the project or assets are already planned and government subsidies are available, the decision to use this form of financing is quite an easy one. However, if the investment in the project or assets is marginal, then the analysis must first include the benefits of the lower cost financing before the evaluation is finalized.

Tax benefits can be reflected in the analysis and evaluation process in a most direct manner. As with any type of tax effect, future cash inflows should be increased for the reduction in tax rates. Yet, the benefit of low-interest loans from the government or a bank should be incorporated as a change in the investment itself.

The change in financing costs is really equivalent to a change in the original commitment that is made by the subsidiary and, thus, by its multinational corporation parent. Therefore, the lower interest rate can reduce the debt element in the weighted-average cost of capital. (See the discussion in Chapter 7 on adjusting the cost of capital for government subsidies in the evaluation of foreign capital expenditures.) This lower cost of capital can be used as an easy benchmark, against which a project's return on investment can be compared, or as a lower discount rate to raise the present value of the project.

Similarly, the reduced investment commitment involved in the lower interest rate can be shown even more directly and more significantly by taking the present value of the interest rate benefits, discounted at the corporation's normal cost of debt, as the reduction in the initial investment in the project. The following example demonstrates this approach:

- Loan amount = $10 million
- Maturity = ten years
- Normal posttax cost of debt = 5 percent
- Subsidized posttax interest rate = 2 percent
- Present value of benefits = present value at 5 percent of $300,000 ten-year annuity = $2.3 million

In some countries, we have even seen a combination of both lower interest and tax benefits in the form of tax-driven leases. One example is the leases used in the recent past to encourage local film production in the United Kingdom. British creditors could become lessors of film rights, obtain tax benefits, and pass them on through a low interest rate implicit in the lease. Sometimes similar benefits are unintentionally created through the structure of local tax laws. We have seen several types of leases considered for various types of assets of high-tax-rate Japanese operations.

VARYING REAL INTEREST RATES

As discussed in Chapter 8, the real dollar-equivalent interest rates may be high or low in some countries at different times. This is especially true in hyperinflationary countries.

If these real rates are projected to be high or low for all or a major portion of the financing period, borrowing in the local market or in the local currency can become especially unfavorable or favorable. If high real interest rates are a function of political risk, blocked funds risk, or expropriation risk, local borrowing may still be considered preferable (see Chapter 12). However, if there is no relationship of the interest rates to the level of risk beyond that of doing business in the country, which is already being taken by having a subsidiary operation in the country, selection of local borrowing should be preferred if the real interest rates are low and should be replaced by nonlocal borrowing combined with intercompany loans or equity contributions if real interest rates are high.

RELATIONSHIP TO RISK MANAGEMENT

Local currency debt is one of the devices cited in Chapter 12 as a preventive measure against the risk of both foreign exchange rate changes and the possibility of funds becoming blocked.

With respect to foreign exchange rates, forecasts of future exchange rates or the alternative of forward market contracts must be considered to determine the dollar-equivalent interest rates. These are the primary criteria for the selection of the currency and, possibly, the market in which debt funds are to be obtained.

Yet, for risk transfer, a premium interest rate may prove

worthwhile, as previously shown. In this case, the magnitude of the estimated risk measured against the interest rate differential becomes the primary criterion for evaluation of local loans. Of course, this assumes that the risk involved will actually be transferred to the local lender or government by the use of local borrowing. However, the latter is not true in the following cases:

- **Matched-fund loans are involved**—if there is a legal right of set-off in the country where the matched-fund loan is made by the corporation as the lender.
- **Parental guarantees are given**—which will still be valid under the laws of the parent's country.
- **A nonlocal bank is the lender to the subsidiary**—but most corporations will honor such loans, even if there is a problem with the local government and a local branch of the bank made the loan. (Yet, some protection is still provided against blocked funds, if the subsidiary has the cash and the ability under local law to repay the local branch, and if the loan agreement does not call for payment in another country.)

SUMMARY AND CONCLUSIONS

While the choice of equity versus debt funding of foreign subsidiaries is a special capital structure decision, the choice of the market and the currency for debt financing may rest on different grounds.

The first goal is to use local cash balances and local cash flows that are generated to avoid the buildup of excess cash on both local and consolidated bases, with the interest income earned far below the 25–30 percent cost of capital. In turn, this potential buildup will be more likely where repatriation of funds is blocked or restricted.

Lack of internal funds is also likely for many subsidiaries in a startup or expansion mode, where lack of cash generated or capital requirements necessitate funding beyond the internal capability of the subsidiary. When parental contributions are deemed inadvisable, other debt sources must be sought. Formal intercompany loans or informal extensions of trade credit are often the easiest forms of such debt and offer many of the same funding, long-term foreign exchange, and risk attributes as equity contributions to the subsidiary.

External local debt taken out by the subsidiary is the next major alternative.

Four major categories of local debt are commonly used:

- **Bank loans**
- **Bank lines of credit**
- **Loans from other multinational corporations**
- **Local capital markets**

When local debt is not available to the subsidiary on a standalone basis two mechanisms are often used:

- **Parental guarantees**
- **Matched funding**

Yet, in terms of both risk and the effect on consolidated financial statements, apart from foreign exchange rate changes, these vehicles are also quite similar to equity contributions.

To obtain local debt funds for a financially troubled subsidiary, more favorable terms, or off-balance-sheet accounting treatment, the following asset-related debt can be used:

- **Mortgages**
- **Receivables factoring**
- **Inventory-collateralized loans**
- **Leases**

Even more advantageous borrowing terms can be achieved through government-subsidized, low-interest, or tax-benefited borrowing in some countries. These may merely be a function of tax loopholes, but are often related to the following government goals:

- **Selected project financing**
- **Selected industry support**
- **Selected export increases**

In addition to their obvious effect on financing strategies, these benefits are often significant enough to alter evaluations of the investment proposals themselves:

- **Increased future cash flows from lower taxes**
- **Reduced cost of capital for interest savings** (see Chapter 7)
- **Reduced initial investment for the present value of interest savings** (authors' preferred approach for interest savings, as opposed to tax savings)

The choice of the market or currency in which to borrow external debt funds is related to the subsidiary's target capital structure (see Chapter 8), but is a separate decision, for which two factors must be weighed:

- **Real interest rates**
  —Dollar equivalent rates
- **Risk effects** (see Chapter 12)
  —Expropriation
  —Blocked funds
  —Foreign exchange rate fluctuations

The evaluation of risk transfers for all of the financing alternatives discussed in this chapter must be made in light of the multinational corporation's overall philosophy. For example, in dealing with many international banks, the corporation will support local subsidiary borrowing with or without issuance of a formal guarantee.

FOOTNOTES

1. Krackov, Financing Foreign Operations of Multinational Corporations, *Handbook of International Corporate Finance*, Allen & Unwin, 1989.

2. Krackov & Kaushik, *The Practical Financial Manager*, New York Institute of Finance, A Division of Simon & Schuster, 1988, Chapter 21.

SELECTED REFERENCES

Krackov, Lawrence M., "Financing Foreign Operations of Multinational Corporations," *Handbook of International Corporate Finance*, Allen & Unwin, 1989.

Krackov, Lawrence M. and Surendra K. Kaushik, *The Practical Financial Manager*, New York Institute of Finance, A Division of Simon & Schuster, 1988, Chapter 22.

CHAPTER 10

Managing Cash and Monetary Investments of Foreign Operations

Once a foreign operation is established, capitalized, and financed, the next immediate task of the multinational finance manager is to handle the local cash flow in an efficient manner. As in the United States, this entails acceleration of receipts of cash to the point at which they become available funds earlier at the subsidiary's bank. As in the United States, this also entails deceleration of disbursements to the point at which available funds are removed later from the subsidiary's bank account balances.

CASH FLOW ELEMENTS

Figure 10-1 shows the major elements of any collection disbursement system.[1] The subsidiary operation will act as both a trade-creditor supplier and a trade-debtor customer. Similarly, the subsidiary will become involved with banks as both the payee and payor of bank transfers made by checks, drafts, and wires.

RECEIPT PRACTICES

Credit terms will generally be a matter of negotiation between the suppliers and customers, as they are in the United States.[2]

FIGURE 10-1: *CASH FLOW DIAGRAM*

Payee Mails Invoice		*Payor Releases Check*		*Payee Receives Check*		*Payee Deposits Check*		*Good Value of Funds*
———	Credit terms Negotiated	———	Mail float Mail, pickup, & wire	———	Processing Lockbox or hand deposit	———	Availability Value agreement	———

However, the customary times allowed for payment will vary greatly. In some areas of the world, periods as long as six months are common. Also, in countries in which inflation levels are very high (hyperinflationary countries), delays in mailing payments may be the most important element of income for the customer and the greatest problem for expenses of the supplier.

The payment mechanism is another area in which customer relations have a definite impact on the cash flow. Acceptance of checks by mail is a common practice in the United States. However, in countries such as France and Belgium, drafts or wire transfers are more common; and the effect is obviously to reduce float. Yet, if mail is used, delays could be significantly greater in Third World countries than in the United States or Western Europe.

Once payments are received, they must be moved as quickly as possible to the company's concentration accounts, whose balances determine the amount of investments to be made or funds to be borrowed. Who gets checks and how quickly he or she can deposit them and then move the funds to the concentration accounts are critical. Yet, lock box systems, which expedite the deposit process in the United States, do not appear to be duplicated in other countries. Designation of the employees responsible and the procedures that they must use for receiving and depositing checks are key factors. Also, for all forms of receipts, the local financial manager must avoid maintaining any large balances in the system beyond the concentration account; and he must manage this area on a daily basis.

DISBURSEMENT PRACTICES

Obviously, a company's procedures as a payee are often the flip side of its own policies as a vendor. In countries such as France and Belgium, there may be a trade-off between using mail checks and draft wire transfers. If the latter is a more common business practice, more could be lost in relations with suppliers than gained in interest if the company insists on paying by check. Yet, we have seen at least one major multinational corporation use checks, rather than drafts, to add five to six days' float in France.

In terms of more sophisticated mechanisms, the use of remote clearing banks in the United States does not appear to be duplicated. This is probably due to the business practices in other countries—such as those calling for drafts and wire transfers in France and Belgium or those using only local banks in other countries. It may also be partially due to the national banking systems in other countries, which present a different type of clearing. It could also be a factor of postdating checks, which minimize the effects of clearing times in many countries, especially in Latin America.

Perhaps as important is the use of anticipated funding of disbursements outside of the United States. The more sophisticated, controlled disbursement systems in the United States, however, show the accurate estimated disbursements to be funded and/or allow funding the next day in return for prefunding of the average one-day-lag amounts. This means daily funding can be delayed until required and no cash need be tied up in anticipated funding and a "cushion" balance (see next section).

BANKING PRACTICES

The primary banking considerations that affect cash flow are negotiated availability schedules that determine when cash can be used by the payee or is removed from the payor's account. While this is true in the United States, the availability ranges are wider in and can vary much more widely among other countries. In Latin America, deposit availability can wait as long as five days, versus a maximum of two days in the United States. For disbursement accounts in many countries, charges can actually be made prior to the date on the check to provide normal compensation to the banks. In other words, playing the float may be quite a different game for international checking accounts.

Bank systems also usually lack some of the more sophisticated elements of U.S. cash management systems. In the United States, cleared checks can be made known early in the morning, and negotiations can permit coverage to be made on the following day, with the average overdraft created being funded or borrowed on a monthly basis. Deposits can also be immediately transferred to a concentration account by depository transfer checks, to give availability in the concentration account as soon as availability of the original deposits permit. Finally, any errors in funds use that create a deficit can usually be handled by agreements with the banks for emergency overdraft capabilities. Such mechanisms are usually unavailable in foreign banking systems, even in technologically advanced countries.

A concentration system may not even be fully available in the same manner outside of the United States. A concentration system takes money collected from various sources at different banks, branches, or collection accounts—usually in different cities—and transfers them to one concentration account via wire or depository transfer checks. The total available funds for use in the business or for money market investments by the corporation can be seen at one time in one place. This allows the decision on maximum investments to be made and minimum cash to be retained.

Similarly, different bank accounts in different branches or for different divisions and subsidiaries can be combined in the United States. So overdrafts in one subsidiary account are offset by cash in the other accounts. While such pooling systems can be established in some foreign countries, impediments are quite common, even in Western European countries such as France. (See the bank pooling discussion in Chapter 11.)

On the other hand, national banking in most foreign countries allows bank accounts in different cities to be combined more easily. The major banks usually have their own branches in all major cities within the country, which eliminate the need for depository transfer checks. However, the key factor for comparing the systems may be the existence or lack of bankwide, on-line balance information among all the branch accounts to allow centralized management on a timely basis.

Compensating balances is another major difference encountered in some parts of the world—especially in Asia and Latin America. In the United States, such balances, which had been used to compensate banks, have been replaced by specific prices for individual services to be paid in cash. While earnings credits may be earned for U.S. bank balances in lieu of charges for bank services, this is merely an additional factor as opposed to any normal monetary compensation system. After all, most U.S. treasurers seek to minimize cash balances. They either prefer to utilize funds for higher-interest investments in securities and money market instruments, or prefer to invest all funds in the company's business at the required 25–30 percent pretax required return, thus avoiding any "excess cash" at all.[3]

INVESTMENT POLICY

In selecting financial investments of excess cash, multinational financial managers should attempt to manage their foreign portfolios in a manner analogous to their domestic U.S. policies. For many, this means a conservative safe approach, but safety may be much more difficult to obtain in many countries.

While aggressive investments could include foreign stocks and even U.S. stocks, with the gamble on foreign exchange rates, a conservative approach would seek the safest fixed-income investments in the subsidiary's own local currency. Securities backed by the local sovereign government or A1/P1-rated commercial paper are the most promising. Yet, practically speaking, deposits at one of the largest and safest local banks is the only conservative investment that can be expected in many cases.

A conservative approach may also seek short maturities of six months or less. This could be even more true for foreign operations if repatriation through dividends or intercompany loans is a possibility (see Chapter 11). Again, just as compensating balances that fail to earn the required 25–30 percent U.S. dollar-equivalent return, so usually does any investment of cash in monetary instruments rather than in the company's own business. The preservation of every opportunity to repatriate such cash and invest it in the business in other countries or to use the cash to retire debt or repurchase stock in the parent company's home country is obviously a major consideration of foreign cash management.

The other difference in foreign portfolios are the risks inherent in placing cash in any investments in some countries. For example, both political and economic problems could make some government obligations risky. Similarly, even the banking system's safest members in some countries are far from safe if the overall governments of the countries are in jeopardy. It is often advisable to seek, but difficult to obtain, a letter of guarantee or comfort from the parent owner of a local bank when the parent is located in the United States or a similarly safe economy. Where such a safeguard is available, however, it would protect any deposit at the local bank or any government security purchased through the local bank.

ARBITRAGE POLICY

One final consideration for local cash management must be described. Many local financial managers seek arbitrage situations in which they can borrow from one portion of their market, such as a bank, and invest the money at a higher rate in another portion of the market. Usually, of course, the higher rate reflects higher risk, just as it does in the efficient U.S. markets. However, this is not always true in the foreign arena, especially for U.S. multinational corporations.

For example, a few years ago, a surprising situation developed in Germany, where U.S. corporations could borrow money more cheaply than the rate paid on German government securities. Therefore, some U.S. corporations borrowed money in Germany and reinvested the funds in the higher-yielding government securities. Initially, it appeared that the accountants would allow both the "riskless" asset and the debt to be netted and reflected at zero on the balance sheet. The interest rate spread would be left as additional income, without any additional capital investment. When this was true, it was a good deal.

Now, however, it appears that the accountants will force any such increase in capital to be reflected on the balance sheet. Thus, even the 50 basis-point interest rate spread shown in Table 10-1 represents a poor marginal return—such as the increase from 8 percent to only 8½ percent, when a 25–30 percent return was required by the parent corporation.[3]

SUMMARY AND CONCLUSIONS

The goals of managing local foreign cash flows for a multinational corporation are very similar to the goals of any American corporation operating in the U.S. marketplace. Within the con-

TABLE 10-1: *ARBITRAGE EXAMPLE*

German interest rate spread	
Corporate borrowing rate	5 percent
German government security rate	$5^1/_2$ percent
Spread	50 basis points
Dollar-equivalent incremental returns	
Money market rate	8 percent
Return with German arbitrage spread	$8^1/_2$ percent
Required return on capital	25–30 percent
Consolidated capital increased by full amount of German borrowings	

straints of customer and supplier relations, receipts should be accelerated and disbursements should be delayed to increase the cash generated. Then the banking systems and negotiated procedures should maximize the speed at which cash becomes available in the corporation's concentration accounts, while delaying to the extent possible the speed at which disbursements are charged against the corporation's account. This maximized cash balance should then be invested in instruments as safe as those that would be required in the United States to maintain availability for investing in the business or repatriating the funds when excess cash persists.

The actual implementation of this rather basic approach in cash management and investment can vary greatly in different countries. For example, wire transfers, bank drafts, and postdated checks may be widely used in some countries, unlike in the United States. Also, the lock-box-receipt and remote-clearing-disbursement systems, commonly used in the United States, are not duplicated abroad. Both local business practices and national banking systems are two of the major reasons for this.

The differences continue into investment decisions, with the required redefinition of "safety" as merely a relative term in many countries. Also, shorter maturities may be more desirable, with a view toward repatriation and potential use of local excess cash in other operations of the multinational corporation.

FOOTNOTES

1. Krackov, "International Cash Management for a Multinational Corporation," *Working Paper* (Institute of International Banking, Pace University, 1987), p. 3.
2. Krackov, p. 2.
3. Krackov, p. 6.

SELECTED REFERENCES

Abdullah, Fuad A., *Financial Management for the Multinational Firm,* Prentice-Hall, 1987, Chapter 8.

Eiteman, David K. and Arthur I. Stonehill, with a contribution by Donald R. Lessard, *Multinational Business Finance,* Addison-Wesley, Fourth Edition, 1986, Chapter 15.

Krackov, Lawrence M., "International Cash Management for a Multinational Corporation," *Working Papers,* Institute of International Banking, Pace University, 1987.

Levi, Maurice, *International Finance,* McGraw-Hill, 1983, pp. 1–460, Chapter 10.

Shapiro, Alan C., *Multinational Financial Management,* Allyn and Bacon, Second Edition, 1986, Chapter 10.

CHAPTER 11

Repatriation and Transfers of Cash from Foreign Subsidiaries

The most important goal of international cash management is to bring home excess cash that is not needed for fixed and working capital investments in the business. If excess cash earns only an 8 percent U.S. dollar-equivalent return, this must be compared with repatriated cash, which should be invested in the corporate business in the United States or worldwide at the standard 25–30 percent expected and required return. Even if it is not invested, it can be used to retire debt or stock at home in the United States, with the same 25–30 percent return effect. The 25–30 percent return rate is merely the pretax equivalent of the approximately 15 percent posttax hurdle rate range used by most companies.

DIVIDENDS FROM SUBSIDIARIES

Dividends and intercompany fees are the two major vehicles for repatriating foreign cash. Intercompany loans can also be used to simulate the effect of dividends. Under some transfer pricing policies, intercompany sales of goods or intangible rights can also be used to simulate intercompany fees, but the company can rarely do this while remaining within the legal requirements of an arm's-length transaction.

The legal restrictions on dividends usually involve the retained earnings levels and minimum capital stock levels of the foreign subsidiary. In other words, you may not repatriate money that was the minimum amount necessary to establish the subsidiary until more money is earned or until the subsidiary is liquidated and dissolved.

In addition to the legal restrictions, we have seen as many constraints imposed on major corporations by the political and psychological situations with their own management or local governments. These issues were discussed in Chapter 8 with respect to the capital structures of foreign subsidiaries. As stated there, the dividend philosophy and strategy are to a great extent the offshoot of the capital structure approach coupled with the local cash generation capability of the operation after satisfaction of local capital investment needs.

Procedurally, dividends must be declared by the subsidiary to the parent entity. The latter is usually the parent company's home country, such as the United States, a holding company in the worldwide organization, or a local holding company for all the corporation's operations in the given country. Ultimately, the dividends will be declared to the entity that can properly utilize the funds on behalf of the overall organization, as described above.

Remittance of the dividends is then made of the declared amounts. Of course, the payments are reduced by any required withholding taxes, which may or may not be recoverable. The declaration and remittance are often performed simultaneously to avoid creating additional foreign exchange exposure under U.S. generally accepted accounting principles (GAAP).

INTERCOMPANY LOANS

In line with our primary goal of bringing home cash, excess liquidity that cannot be repatriated through dividends and fees can be made available for the use of the overall organization by intercompany loans from cash-rich subsidiaries to the parent company.

From an accounting perspective, loan payables and receivables are eliminated upon consolidation of the corporate books.

See how the $100 of excess assets at the subsidiary can be reduced to $50 on a consolidated basis in Figure 11-1.[1]

Intercompany loans are usually much less controversial than dividends in terms of dealings with local management and the local subsidiary capital structure. The loans remain assets of the subsidiary and continue to earn interest. Thus, from the foreign perspective, one monetary investment is merely substituted for another.

In countries in which the multinational corporation has a bank pool or cash concentration system covering more than one subsidiary, the same effect as an intercompany loan can automatically be achieved—as long as the overall pool has more cash than overdrafts and some local funding is needed. This can be seen in Figure 11-2, where $200 of excess cash in the subsidiary can be cut in half by merely funding the corporate needs with a bank overdraft that nets against the cash balances.

Another benefit of either a bank pool or an intercompany loan is avoidance of paying an outside creditor, such as a bank or bondholder, a higher rate on borrowed funds than the rate earned by the corporation on excess cash. Yet, the real savings in avoiding

FIGURE 11-1: *INTERCOMPANY LOANS TO PARENT*

Before loan

Subsidiary Asset	*Parent Debt*	*Consolidated Balance Sheet*	
Cash $100	Comm. paper $100	Cash $100	Comm. paper $100

After loan

Subsidiary Asset	*Parent Debt*	*Consolidated Balance Sheet*	
Cash $50	Comm. paper $50	Cash $50	Comm. paper $50
Loan to parent $50	Loan from subsidiary $50		

FIGURE 11-2: *BANK POOL*

Corporate Account	
	Overdraft $100

CBS Account	
Net cash $100	

Division Account	
Cash $200	

excess cash and capital is much higher—namely, the 25–30 percent return in the business versus the 8 percent return on cash.

Going one step further, we could reach the ultimate in international cash management. Regional or worldwide bank pools are possible where cash in one country offsets overdrafts in the United States that are used to zero out excess foreign cash. Yet, such mechanisms still appear to be somewhat in the future. Some of our exploratory discussions with banks have raised the following problems with respect to global pools: requirements with respect to individual country laws, accounting for one pooled bank account in more than one country, and the limitation in selecting foreign banks that must be affiliates of one worldwide bank.[2]

As a practical matter, intercompany loans should be limited to subsidiaries whose cash exists over the life of the loan. Otherwise, additional borrowing will result for the overall corporation through the subsidiary to offset any efficiency in the use of excess liquidity by the parent.

After cash forecasts are made, the next step is to ascertain which countries allow such loans and any restrictions as to maturities or interest rates. Also, if there are any nonrecoverable withholding taxes on the interest, these must be factored into the net savings computation, which will certainly reduce the spread between the 8 percent level interest and the required 25–30 percent return.

INTERCOMPANY FEES

The other major source of repatriated funds, along with dividends, is intercompany fees. Management fees, consulting fees, technical charges, travel and entertainment reimbursement charges, and so on, all fall within its category. Some analogous payments may also be treated in the same manner—that is, by having the subsidiary host a conference for the overall corporate organization.

While such fees may be affected by internal political and psychological considerations, they are less prone to major arguments than are dividends. Also, such repatriation procedures are often established quite early in the life of a new subsidiary as one of its fundamental operating concepts, whereas dividends are more flexible and are subject to annual review and internal negotiations.

Of course, there are the usual caveats with respect to government regulations. Obviously, if the fees are not viewed as part of legitimate, normal arm's-length transactions, the local foreign governments will dispute and prohibit the transfer of funds to the parent organization that would be viewed as circumventing dividend and intercompany loan regulations.

Ideally, the subsidiary businesses will generate the funds for the fees; thus, the fees are really absorbing excess cash. Yet, even if local debt is temporarily required to pay the fees or if past-due credit terms from the parent are temporarily required to finance the fee obligations, the long-run effects should be an efficient repatriation mechanism. As stated above, this will prevent the buildup of low-return excess cash and capital over time.

INTERCOMPANY SALES AND TRANSFER PRICING

In some cases, one other major type of intercompany transaction and transfer payment can also be considered a form of repatriation. Intercompany sales of the parent company's products and services to a foreign subsidiary are often a fundamental part of doing business in a given foreign country. The products and services will ultimately be resold to foreign customers or will be used in the local production process to manufacture finished goods, which will then be sold to foreign customers.

The economics of the business usually involve a certain profit potential for given products or services that can be earned by the corporation. The choice of providing some parts or services at the parent level as opposed to the local foreign subsidiary level can certainly affect this profit potential. Yet, once the manner of doing business is established, the given profit potential will then merely be divided between the parent and the foreign subsidiary. This division of profit will be implemented through transfer pricing.

For domestic businesses, transfer pricing is a complex, controversial, and somewhat subjective topic. In fact, since no piece of an overall corporation is the same as an independent company, there is no one correct method of establishing transfer prices. While both market prices and cost-plus prices have significant benefits, the real goal is to maximize the combined overall profit for the corporation.[3]

However, international transfer prices deal with separate entities in separate countries. In this situation, market-level transfer prices that simulate an arm's-length transaction are usually required. Obviously, governments do not want income transferred from their countries for various legal and tax reasons.

Nevertheless, a market-level transfer pricing policy can usually determine merely a range of actual prices. Within that range, some discretion may exist. Apart from obvious tax considerations—of generating more income in lower-net-tax-rate countries—one of the primary considerations can be the incremental repatriation that can result. In other words, discretion can be used to simulate the effect of intercompany fees by establishing a higher transfer price and shifting more profit and payments to the parent organization.

GENERAL CROSS-BORDER TRANSFERS AND FOREIGN CURRENCY CONVERSIONS

To repatriate cash or make any other international payments, there must usually be a transfer of funds across a border and a conversion of funds into a different currency. Unlike the domestic or individual foreign country movements of cash, different sovereign nations are involved because funds transfers must comply with their government regulations, which are often restrictive. In addition, even payments to members of the corporate organization are covered by restrictive regulations. In fact, the different entities within the corporate organization have all been set up with a view toward tax, legal, or political considerations. Restrictive regulations burden the transfer process with meeting the legal basis and paperwork documentation requirements.

Internal procedures as well as government relations may also be complicated when funds transfers require conversion to another currency. For many currencies, it is possible to make the conversion through a major interbank market—such as New York or London. Then it may be preferable for the parent staff to do this for all major foreign exchange purchases. However, for small transactions, it is often more convenient to use subsidiary relationships with local banks and to delegate authority for some spot transactions to subsidiaries. For countries with particularly restrictive foreign exchange conversion regulations, such as those in Latin America, central bank involvement is required; foreign exchange purchases by the local subsidiary, with or without local legal counsel, are probably the most efficient procedure. Finally, in cases in which the foreign currency rate fluctuation exposure is hedged with forward contracts, it is sometimes efficient merely to take delivery of the currency under the forward contracts, rather than to purchase a separate spot contract.[4]

NETTING SYSTEMS

Greater overall efficiency for regional groups of subsidiaries can be obtained through a regional netting system. For example, many multinational corporations net payments among all of their operations in Europe. Instead of direct payments from one subsidiary to another and from each subsidiary to the parent company, all the payments of each entity to and from all the other entities are netted. As shown in Figure 11-3,[5] in bilateral netting, the $1,000 payment to the French subsidiary is partially offset by the $500 payment to the Holland subsidiary, so only one payment of $500 must be made.

In multilateral netting, even greater efficiency can be achieved. The five net payments in Figure 11-4,[6] totaling $1,900 among four entities, are converted to three net payments, totaling

FIGURE 11-3

Bilateral Gross

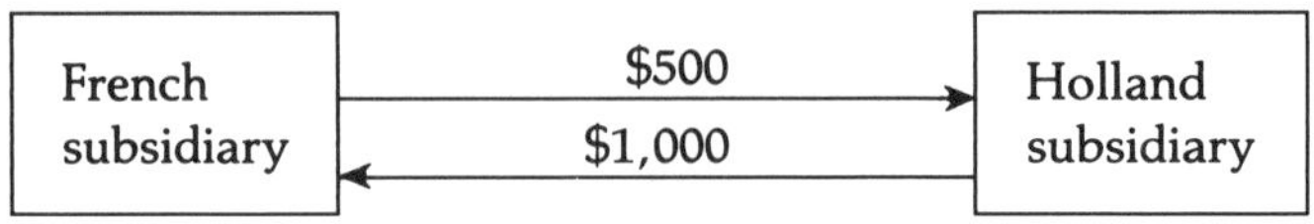

Bilateral Netting

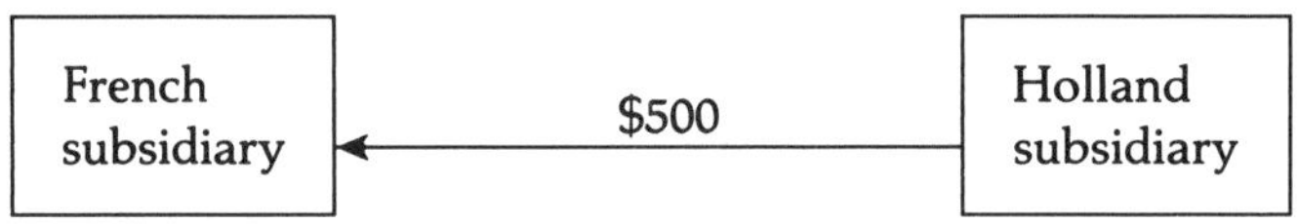

only $800, made to the central bank of the system. For most corporations, this central bank is located in London or Amsterdam.

Thus, not only are gross payable and receivable payments netted, but payments to different subsidiaries are further netted.

Netting of cross-border payments provides three benefits: First, there is a significant reduction in the number of foreign exchange purchases and in their associated transaction costs. Second, netting provides the corporation with an opportunity to obtain more competitive quotes on larger (combined) foreign exchange purchases. Third, this type of system gives the parent the ability to provide all of its subsidiaries with receipts and disbursements in their own local currencies.

Some companies also utilize such a netting system to lag large payments in different currencies as an exposure management device. (We will cover foreign exchange exposure management separately in Chapter 13, where we will show how it can be handled by a better but more complex system that uses a large number of forward contracts annually.) Similarly, leading and lagging can transfer liquidity by automatically financing one subsidiary through a buildup of its intercompany account with another subsidiary. (Local financing and the use of intercompany accounts were discussed in Chapter 9, and we feel that these should also be handled in totally separate analyses.) The netting system that is described here

FIGURE 11-4

Multilateral Direct

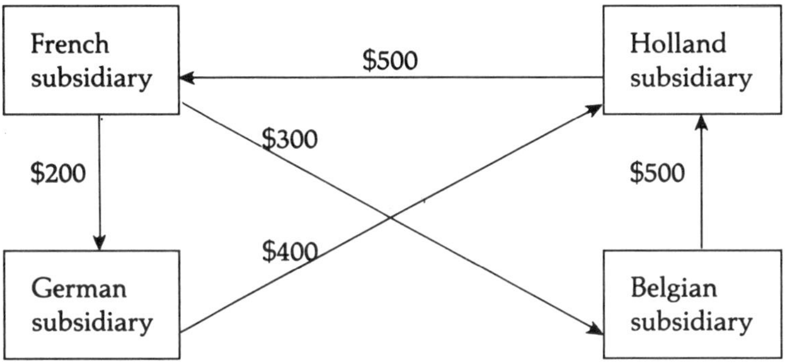

Multilateral Netting

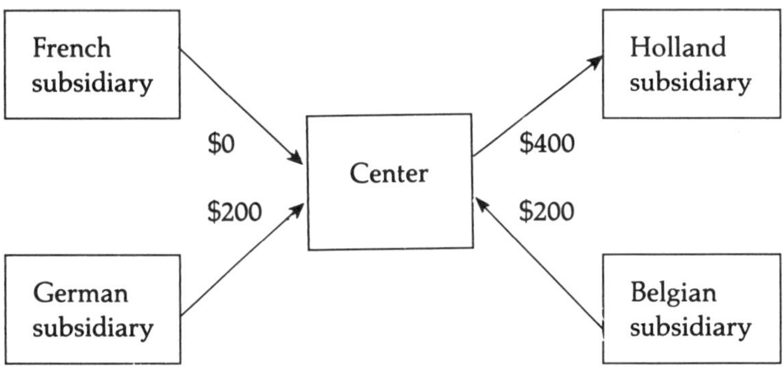

merely makes payments more efficiently. The decision to make the payments should have been made for various reasons by the divisions and subsidiaries or by the international treasury operations department.

REGIONAL FINANCE CENTERS

Just as netting systems can be embellished to satisfy some foreign currency exposure management and local financing needs, another financial vehicle that is related to cross-border funds transfers can similarly be used. A regional center can optimize financing and foreign exchange exposure for the entire region. As previously stated, a regional netting system can incorporate leads and lags in cash payments to transfer liquidity or modify foreign exchange exposures. An additional set of "bells and whistles" could similarly be added by making the regional center a reinvoicing operation or a captive finance company.

A reinvoice center can redenominate invoices and their related payables and receivables in the subsidiaries' local currencies. The center pays all nonlocal invoices—for suppliers, fees, royalties, etc.—which are denominated in the currency of the payee. Then the center rebills the foreign subsidiaries in their currencies. All foreign exchange exposure is concentrated in the center, where it can be identified and managed more easily through external financing and leading/lagging, as well as with forward contracts.

If liquidity exists within the overall region, the center's credit terms can be used to finance subsidiaries that need credit when they need it. Financing for subsidiaries that do not need it can similarly be reduced when they have adequate cash. This type of trade financing of subsidiaries can easily transfer liquidity from cash-rich to cash-poor operations whenever needed.

For example, see how the finance center in Figure 11-5 retains the L 200 payables for 30 days owed by the French and German subsidiaries to a third-party supplier in the United Kingdom. Yet, both subsidiaries' payables are converted to French francs and Deutsche marks, respectively. Also, the French subsidiary's liquidity needs are financed by an increase of 20 days in credit terms. This, in turn, is funded by the German subsidiary's liquidity through a reduction of 20 days in credit terms.[7]

If the overall region needs to borrow, it can do so through the use of the regional center as a captive finance company. The center would borrow and then either directly lend money to subsidiaries in need or use the leads and lags discussed above to provide them with liquidity. Thus, both external financing for the group and allocation of financing for all the subsidiaries can be managed centrally.

Another alternative for many of the same purposes is a factoring center. Factoring of subsidiary receivables can be used for both exposure management and the transfer of liquidity.

FIGURE 11-5: *REINVOICE CENTER*

Normal Trade Payables to Supplier in the U.K.	*Reinvoice Center*
French subsidiary L 100 30 days	French subsidiary payables Fr 900 50 days
German subsidiary L 100 30 days	German subsidiary payables DM 300 10 days
	Reinvoice center L 200 payables Average 30 days Fr 900 and DM 300 receivables Average 30 days

Since both foreign exchange and interest income and expense are obviously somewhat shifted in all forms for this type of finance center, some tax advantages may also be available. For such reasons, low-tax countries are often selected as the domicile for a finance center. Therefore, tax experts should be contacted before any location or structure is finalized.

While many corporations utilize such a reinvoice or captive finance center, if there is already a centrally managed foreign exchange exposure management system in the parent company or in the region and excess cash exists within the region, a simpler netting system may be more desirable and much cheaper to operate. If there is already a centrally managed foreign exchange exposure management system in the parent company or in the region and excess cash exists within the region, there is no need to establish and staff a separate office for the rebilling and centralized finance functions. The existing staff can set up the netting system.

SUMMARY AND CONCLUSIONS

The primary goal of repatriations is to keep the overall organization's worldwide cash used most efficiently in one of two ways. First, it should be invested in the business by the parent company in the United States or by one of the foreign subsidiaries whenever the returns are greater than the capital employed. Second, it can be used to return funds to the suppliers of capital—the creditors and shareholders—by retiring debt of the parent in the United States or of the foreign subsidiaries or by repurchasing the parent company's stock.

When cash is generated by any subsidiaries and is not repatriated above its local reinvestment requirements, it yields low returns as excess cash. This low-return capital, therefore, should become one of the primary targets for elimination by the treasurer through increased repatriation. The four major vehicles that he can use are dividends, intercompany loans, intercompany fees, and intercompany sales through discretionary transfer pricing.

However, repatriation as well as any other form of cross-border cash payments involves foreign currency conversion and compliance with strict regulations and documentation requirements of the various foreign governments. For greater efficiency, regional netting of cross-border transfers can be made at some designated point in a given time period.

Embellishments of a netting system can also be used for foreign exchange rate exposure management and for leading and lagging of payments to finance local subsidiaries. Going one step further, a regional finance or reinvoice center can provide the same or better services plus a way to finance the overall region's cash needs. Yet, we view local financing and foreign exchange exposure management as separate areas, as discussed in Chapters 9 and 13. Therefore, we prefer to view international cash transfers and netting systems as merely efficient mechanical implementations of other financial strategies of the multinational corporation—that is, repatriation, local financing, and foreign exchange exposure management, and so on.

FOOTNOTES

1. Krackov, "International Cash Management for a Multinational Corporation" (a working paper for the Institute of International Banking, Pace University, 1987), p. 16.

2. Krackov, p. 17.
3. Krackov and Kaushik, *The Practical Financial Manager* (New York Institute of Finance, A Division of Simon & Schuster, 1988), Chapter 5.
4. Krackov, p. 7.
5. Krackov, p. 8.
6. Krackov, p. 9.
7. Krackov, p. 14.

SELECTED REFERENCES

Abdullah, Fuad A., *Financial Management for the Multinational Firm*, Prentice-Hall, 1987, Chapter 6.

Eiteman, David K. and Arthur I. Stonehill, with a contribution by Donald R. Lessard, *Multinational Business Finance*, Addison-Wesley, Fourth Edition, 1986, Chapter 15.

Krackov, Lawrence M., "International Cash Management for a Multinational Corporation," *Working Papers*, Institute of International Banking, Pace University, 1987.

Krackov, Lawrence M. and Surendra K. Kaushik, *The Practical Financial Manager*, New York Institute of Finance, A Division of Simon & Schuster, 1988, Chapter 5.

Rodriguez, Rita M. and E. Eugene Carter, *International Financial Management*, Prentice-Hall, Third Edition, 1984, Chapter 9.

PART IV

PROTECTION OF CAPITAL OF FOREIGN CORPORATIONS

The last group of financial decisions for the multinational corporation concern the elimination of risks involved with their investments and transactions in foreign countries and/or in foreign currencies. Profits that are generated can be eliminated by the effects of changes in foreign exchange rates on revenues and costs. Profits that are generated in a foreign country can also become meaningless if the funds are blocked within that country and the corporation has no local uses for the funds. These risks are among the most significant problems for corporate management, and at times they have made the international business transactions and investments appear too risky for participation by their corporations—especially for U.S.-based management.

The risks can be best prevented, or at least limited, at the time when the investments and transactions are first structured; and such techniques are discussed in Chapter 12. Yet, the remaining risks involving foreign exchange rate fluctuation exposures can still be managed to reduce or eliminate them, as discussed in Chapter 13. Similarly, the remaining risks that ultimately result in blocked funds can still be managed through various repatriation techniques in many cases, as discussed in Chapter 14.

Once the foreign exchange rate and blocked fund risks are controlled and managed to an acceptable level, then the multinational corporation can confidently participate in many international markets without undue fear. Indeed, this may be the most important role for multinational financial managers, given the increasing opportunities and requirements for such participation in the increasingly globalized economic environment in which their firms operate.

CHAPTER 12

Preventing Risks of Foreign Exchange Rate Fluctuations and Blocked Funds

Whenever the multinational corporation engages in an international business transaction, risks related to the exchange of currency must always be considered as primary criteria for the evaluation of the deal.

DESCRIPTION OF THE PROBLEM

One or both of two types of currency exchange risks may be present. First, the transaction may be denominated in a foreign currency, at least from the perspective of the multinational parent or subsidiary. Fluctuations in exchange rates could then make funds to be received or paid by the multinational corporation or merely the assets and liabilities of its subsidiaries much less valuable or more costly in terms of the functional currency of the company.

Second, the transaction may involve funds received directly from a foreign country or generated by the subsidiary to be repatriated; and the transfer may not be allowed by the local government for political or economic reasons. The cash and other assets could then build up in the foreign country well beyond any local need or use for them by the multinational corporation or its subsidiary.

Therefore, in the establishment of business structures on the front end, measures to prevent or limit these risks should always be considered. The process is analogous to any good drafting process for any business contract, which identifies potential problems—what could go wrong in terms of future problems or nonperformance—and the structural changes that can be made in the contract to prevent or lessen the risk. More specifically, there are five types of structural decisions that can be involved:

- **Sales and payment contract structures**
  —Where and how are funds to be paid
  —In what currency funds are to be paid
- **Legal entity structure**
- **Capital structure**
- **Debt financing structure**
  —In which country funds are sourced
  —In which currency debt is denominated
- **Investment portfolio of business and assets**
  —Where to invest
  —In which currency monetary assets are held

Some of the basic structural decisions of these types will be applied to the major international business decisions in this chapter. Many have already been discussed indirectly in previous chapters and these will now be discussed more fully in this chapter.

IMPORT PRICE NEGOTIATIONS

When the multinational parent or subsidiary imports new materials for its manufacturing operations or goods for resale, obvious foreign exchange rate risk is borne by either the company or the seller. If the latter is unaware of the issue, then the goal will be to have the contract price denominated in the multinational's functional currency. Yet, if the seller is a reasonably sophisticated business professional—which is the best assumption to use for most negotiations—there is little chance to sneak such a risk transfer into the sales agreement. Therefore, the risk transfer will usually become one of the more explicit elements of the negotiating process.

The corporation, as the purchaser, should request alternative bids or prices in both the seller's currency (or a third currency of its choice) and the multinational parent's or subsidiary's own functional currency. The combination of the purchase price in the other currency and a forward foreign exchange contract can then be evaluated in the company's functional currency. This amount can then be compared with the functional currency bid to ascertain which bid is preferable.

The following example may help illustrate this concept and procedures:

- **Purchase order options**
  —Japanese robotics equipment grouping
  —Dollar price of $1 million listed
  —Yen price alternative of 115 million quoted upon request
  —Five-month delivery date and payment on open account in 30 days
- **Forward hedging alternative**
  —Six-month forward contract rate of ¥120/$
  —Yen-hedged dollar cost
  ¥115 million / 120 = $960 thousand

There should be no difference in a perfect market, where the seller makes the same calculations—unlike in the above example. The seller should set the price in the buyer's functional currency based on its own combination of a forward contract to exchange the buyer's functional currency proceeds into its own currency. Thus, the same price should be offered to the buyer in terms of its own currency, regardless of the currency in which the sale is denominated.

Yet, some sellers—just as some buyers—do not have access to

the forward foreign exchange markets. Even those with access may not do their homework and make the necessary calculations and comparisons. In these cases, if the seller is willing to provide different prices in different currencies, one price can certainly be cheaper than the other in terms of the multinational corporation's currency, although the $40,000 or 4 percent savings in the above example may be higher than those available in most deal structures .

EXPORT NEGOTIATIONS

When the multinational corporation becomes the seller of goods or services to foreign countries, it should certainly prepare all price bids along the same lines outlined above. Perhaps the best strategy would be to offer prices in the buyer's currency at a level above that of the forward contract plus local currency. Then, if the buyer chooses this "customized" service, it will be paying a somewhat higher price in foreign exchange-adjusted terms.

By selling products and services in its own functional currency, the multinational will be doing general business in its preferred manner. Yet, for buyers who want to be billed in their own currency, proper use of the forward market can allow this "customized" service without any foreign currency risk to the multinational.

As an exporter, as opposed to an importer, the multinational firm also faces the greater risk of the entire sales proceeds being blocked. The trade mechanisms discussed in Chapter 5 can be quite helpful in this area, especially for a one-time transaction such as a single contract or order for the sale of goods.

The simplest protection for the company is to have the proceeds guaranteed for payment in one of the countries in which the multinational firm can utilize them or from which the multinational knows that remittance is safe. A letter of credit—from one of the multinational corporation's banks or any respected multinational bank in a nonblocked currency country—that becomes confirmed and binding upon delivery of the goods is the safest form of protection.

When the sale of goods or services is part of an overall contract, especially when payments are made on a recurring basis, the contract must specify the site as well as the currency of payment. This has been the standard operating procedure for many major U.S.-based multinational corporations. For example, payment in U.S. dollars may protect a U.S. exporter from exchange rate fluctuations, but the company cannot obtain full use of the dollars if the dollar-equivalent value resides in some blocked foreign bank account. The wording of the contract must show that the latter possibility is a breach of contract, which releases the multinational corporation from any further export obligations (or any continuing licensee arrangement). The company will also be allowed to seek both judicial relief for the breach and any necessary changes in its future commercial activity (such as seeking a new licensee).

CAPITAL INVESTMENT DECISIONS

When the multinational corporation deals with capital investments in foreign subsidiaries as opposed to mere export operations, both the foreign exchange and blocked funds risks become more complex. Still, the best protection can often be afforded on the front end.

When the investment decision is made, the risk of blocked funds can be incorporated into the analytical process in two ways, as discussed in Chapter 7. First, the cash flows projected for the net present value calculation can be shown on a parent company basis as well as on a multinational corporate basis. In other words, the only cash flows that are considered relevant in the parent-company case would be those to and from the parent. Estimated blocked funds would be eliminated from the return calculations. Yet, such a precise estimate of blockages for any specific year may be considered too inaccurate or misleading, even on a projected basis. Therefore, the second alternative approach could be adopted. This would include blocked funds risks in the overall cost of capital adjustment for different risk levels associated with any given investment in any given country.

The risk of foreign exchange rate fluctuations can also be accounted for in the net present value analysis. In fact, it must be included to some extent when the choice is made not to forecast exchange rates or inflation rates but merely to assume that the purchasing power parity theory described in Chapter 7 holds. Obviously, if there is a risk that this general approach will not be realistic for a given country over a given time frame, a sensitivity analysis of explicit foreign exchange rate forecasts can be made.

Therefore, the critical point is that both blocked funds risks and foreign exchange rate fluctuation risks must be addressed in our analytical framework. However, the real decision is whether these risks are being adequately handled in our normal approach to using the multinational corporate cash flows and purchasing power parity inflation exchange rate assumptions.

FOREIGN SUBSIDIARY CAPITAL STRUCTURES

Another decision that can be handled on the front end is the choice of a subsidiary capital structure that will assist in the prevention of both blocked funds and exchange rate risks. The minimum equity approach for establishing the capital structure—which is discussed at length in Chapter 8—is primarily aimed at maintaining maximum flexibility to avoid the buildup of local cash and the possibility of blocked funds. An additional benefit of this approach is the discouragement or prevention of increases in assets and the related foreign exchange exposure.

Minimum amounts of equity allowed by local laws and business customs will logically provide for the maximum amount of local debt in the foreign subsidiary capital structure. This will then give the multinational a way to use the local funds generated: to repay local loans during periods of blocked or restricted foreign payments for the subsidiary. Thus, even when subsidiary dividend payments or intercompany loan repayments are prohibited, local cash levels will not build up when the funds generated by the business are absorbed by legal repayments of local debt.

If the subsidiary is consolidated, such local debt repayment will also reduce the consolidated excess capital levels of debt and equity for the multinational corporation. Thus, the risk of blocked funds or at least its negative effects can be prevented as long as local loan obligations remain. Naturally, a minimum equity philosophy toward foreign subsidiary capital structures makes such periods of local loan obligations last longer.

Minimum equity and maximum local debt will also limit the buildup of net assets and net monetary assets. These net assets represent the foreign exchange translation exposure on an accounting basis in regular (nonhyperinflationary) countries and hyperinflationary countries, respectively. To the extent that the multinational corporation fears such exposure for the balance sheet or income statement, respectively, the minimum equity philosophy toward foreign subsidiary capital structures may also be preferred. From an economic standpoint—not merely an accounting perspective—short-term risks are also involved with net assets, even when purchasing power parity works in the long run. This is especially true for net monetary assets when there are no local inflationary increases in the value of assets (unlike fixed assets such as real estate) to offset depreciation of the currency.

While minimum equity is the only capital structure approach aimed directly at blocked fund and exchange rate risks, the other philosophies discussed in Chapter 8 will also have an impact. To the extent that the other approaches to foreign subsidiary capital structures entail greater or lesser equity levels for a given business at a given stage, the blocked fund and exchange rate risks will be greater or lesser, as discussed above. An example of the resulting debt/capital levels for the different approaches is shown in Table 8-1 in Chapter 8.

Finally, the related decision about the amount of dividends to be paid by the foreign subsidiary to the parent corporation or to a holding company within the multinational corporation should also be made with blocked funds and exchange rate risks in mind. Since high dividends are the flip side of minimum equity, they will tend to limit both of those risks for the same reasons discussed above. Unlike dividends to the ultimate shareholders of the multinational corporate parent—which can increase the risk of inadequate funding or bankruptcy—subsidiary dividends can paradoxically be viewed as more of a financial safeguard than a risk.

FOREIGN SUBSIDIARY FINANCING STRATEGIES

Local debt is the safest form of financing with respect to blocked funds and exchange rate risks, as discussed in the last section. This must be kept in mind when evaluating the specific sources of financing for foreign subsidiaries, as well as the general capital structure to be employed.

From this perspective, local debt should be preferred to an equity contribution from the parent for the initial financing requirements of a new foreign subsidiary or for a new capital project within the subsidiary. Once the business begins to generate cash, the use of higher dividends rather than a low dividend payout ratio should similarly be preferred.

Apart from total equity-versus-debt considerations, local debt should also be used over intercompany loans or trade credits—for transferred products from the parent and other multinational subsidiaries and for fees owed to the parent. As intercompany debt payment capabilities may not hold up in periods of blocked funds, intercompany loans or trade credit are not as safe as local debt from this perspective. Intercompany debt also presents foreign exchange transaction exposure for either the lending or borrowing entity within the multinational corporation. This will remove the benefit of the debt offsetting the foreign exchange exposure of assets being financed.

Local debt also appears safer compared with third-party, nonlocal debt. Blocked funds restrictions may be just as readily applied by a foreign government to any nonlocal payments, regardless of whether the recipient is an affiliated company. Yet, the multinational corporation may be honor-bound or legally bound to make payments due outside of the blocked currency country. Foreign exchange transaction exposure will also be created for the multinational corporation unless the third party accepts debt denominated in the local currency of the subsidiary.

Therefore, while many other considerations must certainly be taken into account in determining the sources of financing to be used, local debt financing is definitely preferred if the primary goal is to prevent funds from becoming blocked or net assets from becoming devalued.

FOREIGN SUBSIDIARY CASH MANAGEMENT AND INVESTMENT STRATEGIES

The decision about how to invest local foreign cash is the reverse of the decision about how to finance local foreign operations.

If financing foreign business with local debt is the safest alternative in terms of avoiding blocked funds and exchange rate risks, investing cash generated by that business in a multinational parent's own home country and in its own hard currency may be the safest strategy. This approach would eliminate some risk of blocked funds, especially in extreme cases of expropriation. This approach would also protect the parent from economic devaluation of its worldwide monetary assets.

However, two practical problems are noted for ongoing businesses. First, the subsidiary may not be capable or desirous of investing outside its home country until the time that funds can be repatriated—through dividends and other mechanisms discussed in Chapter 11. Therefore, one alternative is to use local investments in financial institutions whose own parent companies would provide an external guarantee in case the funds should become blocked. However, as discussed in Chapter 10, such guarantees may be difficult to obtain, although we have seen them in practice.

Second, nonlocal currency investments incur immediate foreign exchange transaction exposure for the local subsidiary. Any resulting foreign exchange losses would then be shown in each period on the income statement.

Thus, in practice, local currency investment of local cash is usually used. Blocked currency risks are addressed through other separate means. Also, if some maxi-devaluation is expected in a hyperinflationary country, exceptions are made and hard currency investments are sought through the government and other multinational companies that need local funds. For example, in Brazil, there are 432 deposits at the central bank and complex exchange rate-adjusted loans from one corporation to another.

In light of the above discussion, perhaps the best strategy on the investment side is merely to maximize repatriation of excess cash and to manage working capital to minimize any noncash buildup of net receivables/payables and inventory beyond local operating needs. The maximization of repatriation, as opposed to external investments of local cash, was discussed more fully in Chapter 11 and previously in this chapter. It depends on the dividend payout ratio selected for foreign subsidiaries as well as the many nondividend alternative mechanisms to return local cash to the overall multinational corporation.

However, even for a maximum dividend approach, local cash investment decisions are required about blocked currency and exchange rate risks. The maturity of local investments, especially those that are illiquid (cannot be traded before maturity), should remain short. This will make all cash more readily available for all forms of repatriation, which is a major part of the investment policy discussed in Chapter 10. We have thus seen it as a bulwark of foreign cash investment policies for several multinational corporations—to keep cash safe and liquid for periodic remittances to the rest of their organizations.

Minimizing the working capital of the business—in the form of receivables not financed by payables and of funds tied up in inventory—may be the best means of providing the maximum cash available for repatriation. This strategy may not only use capital more efficiently, as demonstrated by higher returns on the capital, but may also limit the assets subject to the risks of government blockage and exchange rate exposure. Receivables and payables may be the more important of the working capital elements to be managed by the finance manager. They can be controlled through both the credit/payable accounting policies and collection/disbursement banking systems employed by the subsidiary. The latter can minimize collection float and maximize payables float to maximize cash balances available to the multinational corporation in its bank accounts, which can then be invested or repatriated, as discussed in Chapter 10.

SUMMARY AND CONCLUSIONS

The multinational corporation should stress the consideration of blocked funds risks and exchange rate exposures in its sales/payment contract structures with third parties and in establishment of the financial structure and policies for its own foreign subsidiary operations.

As an importer, the seller may allow the multinational corporation to obtain a lower price if payment is made in a certain manner or in the seller's own currency. While the latter creates an exchange rate exposure for the corporation, it can be covered with forward foreign exchange contracts. Therefore, bids should always be requested in both currencies where there is a forward market.

As an exporter, the corporation must consider the risks of funds becoming blocked by a local foreign government as well as exchange rate exposure. Specifying where and in which currency the payment is to be received and having some bank guarantee that the payment will be made, should provide the necessary protection. If the currency is not the corporation's own functional currency, an additional customer service should be viewed as being provided. Yet, the seller's exposure can also be covered with forward contracts.

When multinational operations are expanded with foreign capital expenditures to establish foreign operations, blocked funds and exchange rates must be taken into account in the financial evaluation, as discussed in Chapter 7. As these operations are financed, both capital structure and financing decisions that greatly impact the potential for blocked funds and exchange rate losses will then be required. Local debt is generally the preferred source of financing for this purpose, since it provides a means to use excess foreign cash, even when cross-border remittances are blocked, and it offsets some of the exchange rate exposure for local subsidiary assets.

However, once local foreign cash is generated, it should be repatriated as soon as possible. Until that time, safe and liquid local investment instruments should be used to maintain the cash available for repatriation. Also, working capital should be managed to minimize receivables and inventory, to maximize payables, to minimize collection float, and to maximize payables float.

CHAPTER 13

Managing Foreign Exchange Exposure for Rate Fluctations

Once the best means are used to prevent, limit, or take into account foreign exchange exposure when establishing business practices and structures, as outlined in Chapter 12, the economic effect of the remaining exposures must be identified and evaluated. Are the remaining exposures worth covering through various hedging techniques, such as purchasing forward contracts, or are they not worth the time and effort involved for both the operating business and treasury department staffs?

EXPOSURES TO CONSIDER AND COVER

At most companies with which we are familiar—and CBS in particular—the type of accounting impact on the financial statements is a key element to consider and should, therefore, be identified. Some exposures always have an impact on the income statement, with the gains and losses being reflected in the foreign exchange line of the income statement. Such exposures should always be hedged with forward contracts, if market conditions allow this to be done efficiently and with relative ease. Yet, if the economic exposures do not have a known impact on the income statement, or if an efficient forward market is lacking, hedging may not be employed. There are three types of indirect accounting exposure at CBS:

- **Undeclared dividends** affect merely expectations, not the consolidated income statement. This is true even if they are specifically designated in the company's formal foreign dividend budget as an input to the domestic cash flow budget of cash available for corporate-level, worldwide spending programs. Thus, such planned dividends are *not hedged, unless* a definite risk is perceived that the entire domestic cash forecast could be significantly reduced by a decline in the dollar-equivalent proceeds from dividends due to strengthening of the dollar exchange rates.
- **Subsidiary earnings** in local currencies may present an exposure for consolidated reported earnings, so they *may be hedged.* If the operating division to which the subsidiary reports feels that it cannot pass on any negative effects of devaluation in the form of local price increases, which will raise local currency revenues and profits to maintain dollar-equivalent income levels, forward contracts are taken out by the corporate treasury department to cover each month's budgeted earnings. We encourage such price increases to be implemented whenever possible, because devaluation is often merely a result of local inflationary pressures.
- **Purchase commitments** in the form of future invoices for imported inventory of raw materials and supplies or for imported equipment *may also be hedged.* The corporate treasury department does this whenever the operating division feels that it cannot pass on local currency devaluation with selling price increases. However, as stated in Chapter 12, the alternative of dollar-denominated price quotes should be considered and obtained whenever possible. These measures will insure fixed dollar-equivalent costs for the purchases.

Given the direct income statement effects discussed previously, the following on-balance-sheet *transaction* exposures are *always hedged* as soon as notice of their booking is received by the corporate treasury department.

- **Receivables** in a foreign currency, including bank deposits and accrued interest.
- **Payables** in a foreign currency, including bank loans and accrued interest.

Conversely, *translation of the net assets* on the local subsidiary balance sheets does not usually have an impact on the foreign exchange line of the income statement, but only on the special equity section of the consolidated balance sheet. Therefore, all such exposures are not hedged with forward contracts. However, for hyperinflationary countries, translation of the net monetary assets gives rise to gains and losses on the foreign exchange line of the income statement. Thus, such exposure could be hedged if approval of the chief financial officer were obtained and if efficient forward markets could be found for such currencies. Recently, the latter have not been available for the Brazilian cruzado, Mexican peso, Argentine austral, and so on.

PROCEDURAL/ORGANIZATIONAL IMPLICATIONS

The approach described above can have the *corporate treasury department* bear all the responsibility for all the *direct accounting impacts* of fluctuations in foreign exchange rates. The treasury department can cover all on-balance-sheet transaction exposures, such as foreign currency-denominated receivables and payables, that have an impact on the foreign exchange line of the income statement.

The *operating divisions* can bear the responsibility of protecting their local dollar earnings from any *indirect effects* of such fluctuations—through pricing actions or requests for hedges. The indirect effects can be on either the local currency profit margins or the dollar-equivalent levels of local currency earnings.

It is obvious with the above responsibilities that the foreign exchange exposure data base and trading must become totally centralized, despite the diversity and decentralization of the operations. This data base must include the largest amounts of foreign

TABLE 13-1: *NET EXPOSURES AND HEDGES*
(thousands of dollars)

	Net Exposure by Division			*Corporate*	*Net*
	A	*B*	*C*	*Hedges*	*Total*
Sterling	$(1,339)	$3,440	$4,156	$(6,257)	$0
Deutsche mark	3,467	0	2,163	(5,630	0
French franc	(193)	0	4,984	(4,791)	0
Italian lira	4,088	0	0	(4,088)	0
Spanish peseta	825	(449)	(7)	(369)	0
Japanese yen	3,198	(1,322)	0	(1,876)	0
Australian dollars	4,625	1,666	401	(6,692)	
Canadian dollars	6,631	1,234	0	(7,865)	0
Other	3,046	0	(135)	(2,911)	0
Total	$24,348	$4,569	$11,562	$(40,479)	$0

exposures designated to be hedged with forward contracts (at CBS, the on-balance-sheet transactions exposure—namely, booked payables and receivables of all types). Payable and receivable amounts in each nonlocal (nonfunctional) currency are reported to the corporate treasury department. They are then consolidated in the corporate computer model to yield worldwide net exposures in each of the major currencies, similar to the simplified summary in Table 13-1.[1]

The net exposure, shown at approximately $40 million in Table 13-1, is offset with forward contracts totaling approximately the same $40 million.

The corporate computer model allows hedging of cross-currency exposures—such as a guilder payable on CBS's German

TABLE 13-2: *FOREIGN CURRENCY EXPOSURES*

	Nonlocal Currency Exposure			*Local Currency*
	$	*G*	*Fr*	*Exposure*
Holland (G)	25	0	150	(100)
France (Fr)	50	100	0	(600)
Total exposures	75	100	150	
Total offsets	0	(100)	(600)	
Net exposures	75	0	(450)	

G/$ = 2.1
Fr/$ = 6.1.

TABLE 13-3: *FORWARD CONTRACT EXPOSURES*

	Nonlocal Currency Exposure		*Local Currency Exposure*
	$	*Fr*	
U.S. $	0	450	(75)
Total exposures	0	450	
Total offsets	75	0	
Net exposures	(75)	450	

books—as well as individual dollar/foreign currency exposures—such as French franc receivable on CBS corporate books in the United States. The long or short position of each exposure in the nonlocal currency is input, and the computer model calculates the local currency offset. Then the net amounts in each currency are calculated and bought or sold forward against the dollar to offset their net short and long positions.

The simplified output form shown in Table 13-2 shows the forward contracts that are required by net short exposures of $75 in French francs.[1]

If a forward contract is then taken out by CBS to purchase FF 450, the net effect would be entered in the same manner, as shown in Table 13-3.[1]

When the hedges and exposures are then consolidated, the net exposure will be totally eliminated, as shown in Table 13-4.[1]

At CBS, the goal is to change the hedge contracts constantly as reported exposures change to keep the net level as close to zero as possible. The net foreign exchange gains and losses are moni-

TABLE 13-4: *NET COVERED EXPOSURES*

	Nonlocal Currency Exposure			*Local Currency Exposure*
	$	*G*	*Fr*	
U.S. $	0	0	450	(75)
Holland (G)	25	0	150	(100)
France (Fr)	50	100	0	(600)
Total exposures	75	100	600	
Total offsets	(75)	(100)	(600)	
Net exposures	0	0	0	

tored to see if they are also close to zero or if there is a problem in the exposure report. If errors are found, the exposure report is corrected.

ALTERNATIVE HEDGE MECHANISMS

In addition to forward contracts, which are more common, there are two other major types of hedge mechanisms that are used to offset foreign exchange exposure that develops in the normal course of international and foreign operations. We are not referring here to the normal cash investment and borrowing/capital structure policies discussed in Chapters 8, 9, 10, and 12, which can lessen the amount of these exposures. Rather, we are referring to the popular techniques of currency options and currency debt swaps.

The currency option is similar to the forward contract in that it allows the multinational corporation to buy (call option) or sell (put option) a given currency for another currency at a specified rate. Naturally, locking in the rate on the front end can be used to hedge changes in exchange rates before maturity of the option contract. Yet, options are used as hedges in most cases only when the amount or existence of an exposure is in doubt.

A perfect example is the hedging of a receipt or payment connected with a project being competitively bid. Since the corporation cannot be sure that its bid will win, the exposure may not exist. Therefore, a forward contract could be quite speculative. Yet, if the corporation wins and the exposure results, some protection may be highly desirable.

If the exposure fails to develop, the only cost of the option is a fixed up-front premium—not the full risk of changes in foreign exchange rates in a forward contract. If the exposure develops, any adverse effect of exchange rate changes can be offset by exercise of the option. Yet, from the multinational corporation's perspective, the option market may not be as efficient as the forward market, in that the initial premium to buy the option from its foreign exchange bank can be high. Moreover, if an accounting emphasis is placed on offsetting only the foreign exchange effects that are reflected on the income statement—as has usually been done at

CBS—the option may not be as easy to set off against the business exposure. This is certainly the case if the exposure does not result, such as in a lost bid situation. Finally, for a large number of deals, the economics of using forward contracts would probably be cheaper in terms of expected values, based on the probabilities of exchange rates changing, by given magnitudes.

For all of these reasons, options have not been used by hyperinflational corporations for hedging as often as their supporters and sellers might have one believe. CBS has never used options, at least in recent years.

While asset translation exposures are usually not hedged by multinational corporations, including CBS, currency debt swaps designated as hedges of net assets are used by corporations to reduce reported interest expense and to increase reported earnings without income statement risk. This was one of the benefits of utilizing international capital markets to improve domestic or worldwide operations, which was discussed in Chapter 6.

Merely swapping U.S. dollar-denominated debt for lower interest rate foreign currency debt saves no interest under the CBS policy, since covering the principal and interest obligations with forward contracts is required to offset the on-balance-sheet transaction exposures thereby created. Then the premium costs on the contracts offset approximately the entire nominal interest savings. See the 11½ percent Eurodollar rate and the 11½ percent forward contract-covered rate in Figure 13-1.

Yet, if the debt swap is made into a currency when net assets are supporting the operations in the currency's home country, the principal of the debt can become a designated hedge of these net assets. In such cases, any foreign exchange gains and losses on that principal will be shown only in the special equity section of the balance sheet and will bypass the income statement. This accounting convention recognizes the fact that, economically, changes in the value of the liability will be offset by changes in the value of the underlying assets. (In other words, as an economist would say, we are merely hedging our economic position.) Therefore, forward contracts required need only cover the interest obligations in the foreign currency. See the 2 percent savings from the Eurodollar rate or the 9½ percent net asset-covered rate in Figure 13-1.[2]

FIGURE 13-1: *FOREIGN CURRENCY/DEBT SWAP*

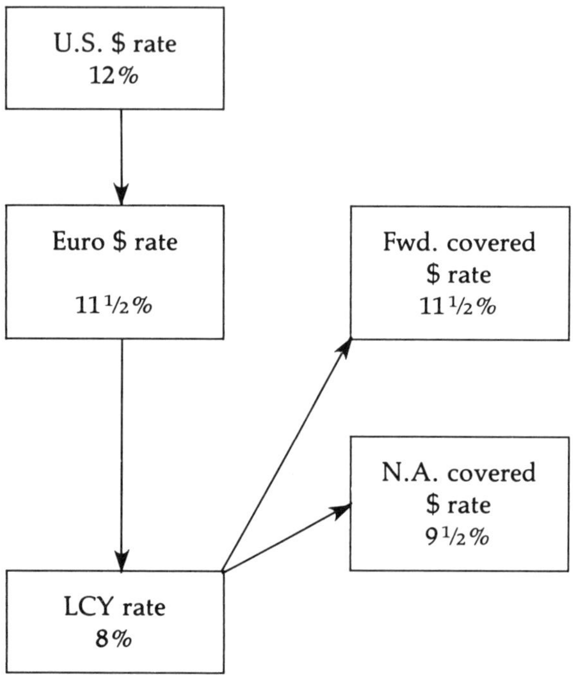

Figure 13-2 shows another currency debt swap that may highlight all the elements of the structure more clearly.[3]

The high 14½ percent dollar interest payments and $60 million of principal (at maturity) are paid to CBS. In turn, the company pays the bank only 8½ percent in foreign currency interest and a principal amount to be determined at the new exchange rate at maturity. The 8½ percent foreign currency interest payments are covered with forward contracts, represented by the box at the top, but the principal exposure is covered without premium costs by the net asset hedge, represented by the box at the bottom.

PHILOSOPHY TOWARD SPECULATION

From the financial strategies shown in Chapters 8, 9, 10, and 12, as well as from the above discussion of hedging policy and pro-

FIGURE 13-2: *CURRENCY/DEBT SWAP STRUCTURE*

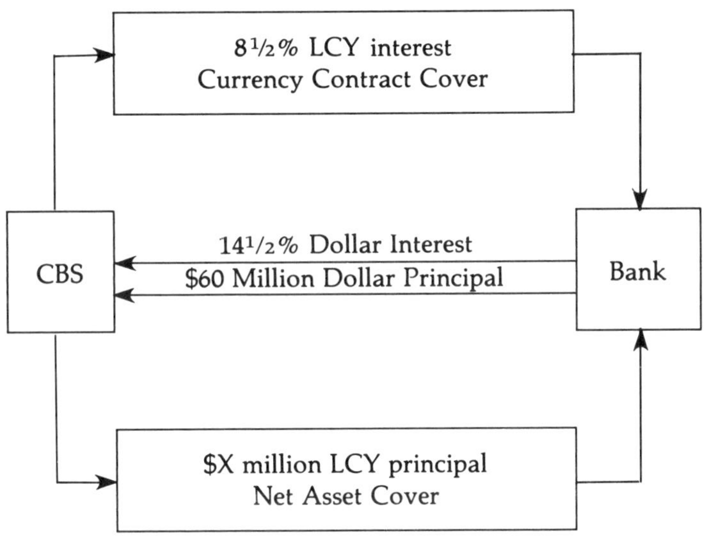

cedures, it is obvious that we are quite negative about speculation on foreign exchange rate changes. We would also use a very comprehensive definition of such speculation, as the taking of any action, based on any forecasts, with respect to foreign exchange rates in the future.

While this philosophy is espoused by many multinational corporations, it is not consistently applied. Instead, three common, but highly speculative approaches have been used by several other nominally antispeculative companies and are often referred to by the foreign exchange trade press:

- **Selective hedging** of only some exposures
- **Partial hedging** of only a portion of the exposure amount
- **Selective removal of hedges** while the exposure still remains

SUMMARY AND CONCLUSIONS

There are many types of foreign exchange rate exposures that can affect the economics of doing business in international markets or through foreign subsidiaries. Yet, for most U.S.-based multinational corporations, the primary criterion used to decide which exposures should be actively managed appears to be the income statement effects that may result.

For example, three categories may be used:

- **Direct income effects** of the following exposures are often hedged:
  —Receivables
  —Payables
- **Indirect income effects** may or may not be hedged, depending on specific circumstances, for the following exposures:
  —Purchase order commitments of buyers and sellers
  —Undeclared dividends from foreign subsidiaries
  —Foreign subsidiary earnings to be translated on the parent's income statement
- **Nonincome effects** are not usually hedged, which explains why net assets in nonhyperinflationary countries are not usually hedged when the accounting rules defer their exchange rate gains and losses in the special equity section of the balance sheet

The organizational implications of this approach may allow the treasury department to hedge all significant direct income effects on a net-exposure-by-currency basis. Yet, the indirect income effects will most probably be hedged on a case-by-case basis, whether centrally or locally.

The best and most widely used mechanism to hedge foreign exchange rate exposures is the forward contract. The currency option is not widely used for hedging, but may be used effectively to cover indefinite exposures, such as those connected with a bidding situation. Currency debt swaps may be used for hedging some exposures by switching debt into offsetting currency positions, but they are more commonly used merely to obtain lower interest rates in low coupon currency debt with designated hedges of net assets in such currencies under the accounting regulations of the Financial Accounting Standards Board's Statement of Financial Accounting Standards No. 52.

The philosophy of most multinational corporations toward hedging is negative, and the approaches outlined in this chapter are in line with this philosophy. Yet, we must be careful to avoid the problem of semantics in this area, and the following three approaches should be avoided as tantamount to speculation:

- **Selective hedging**
- **Partial hedging**
- **Selective removal of hedges**

While conclusions about the empirical results of this type of approach cannot be drawn, the results of the CBS programs that utilized such an approach were favorable. They also demonstrate that the approach can be active, although not speculative.

At one point recently for CBS, the hedge program had attained a 95 percent efficiency in eliminating potential unexpected gains and losses. The less than $1 million in net losses for currencies and operations that is included in the forward contract hedging program could also be attributed solely to premiums paid for low-interest currencies when forward contracts were taken out. These contracts then implicitly allowed more monetary assets to be held in high-interest currencies to earn additional interest income that nearly perfectly offset the premium and discount costs.

In favor of the active side, in a recent three-year period, CBS used 12 currency swaps and 1 foreign currency debt issue with principal amounts exceeding $300 million. It is estimated that cumulatively—over the lives of the 13 transactions, that varied from a few months to ten years—more than $20 million of interest expense savings should have been generated by these designated hedges.

FOOTNOTES

1. Appendix to Foreign Exchange Chapter, *Handbook of International Corporate Finance*, Allen & Unwin, 1989, appendix to Chapter 11.

2. Krackov and Kaushik, *The Practical Financial Manager*, New York Institute of Finance, A Division of Simon & Schuster, 1988, Chapter 17.

3. Ibid., Chapter 14.

SELECTED REFERENCES

Eiteman, David K. and Arthur I. Stonehill, with a contribution by Donald R. Lessard, *Multinational Business Finance*, Addison-Wesley, Fourth Edition, 1986, Chapter 7.

Krackov, Lawrence M., "Financing Foreign Operations of Multinational Corporations," *Handbook of International Corporate Finance*, Allen & Unwin, 1989.

Krackov, Lawrence M. and Surendra K. Kaushik, *The Practical Financial Manager*, New York Institute of Finance, A Division of Simon and Schuster, 1988, Chapter 17.

Riehl, Heinz and Rita M. Rodriguez, *Foreign Exchange and Money Markets*, McGraw-Hill, 1983, Chapter 9.

Shapiro, Alan C., *Multinational Financial Management*, Allyn and Bacon, Second Edition, 1986, Chapters 7 and 9.

CHAPTER 14

Repatriating and Using Blocked Funds

In addition to foreign exchange rate exposure, the other risk discussed in Chapter 12 was blocked funds. While this risk should be considered and prevented to the extent possible, as outlined in Chapter 12, the remaining risk must also be managed. Therefore, the management of blocked funds can be viewed as somewhat analogous to the management of the foreign exchange exposure that remains after reasonable cautionary and preventive measures are taken.

TYPES OF PROBLEMS

The management of foreign exchange rate exposure is hedging, as discussed in Chapter 13. The management of blocked funds is the permanent or temporary repatriation of all or a portion of the funds considered blocked under local laws. These funds can be held by the multinational corporation or can merely be designated to be received by the corporation in a country in which it has no use for the funds; but in either case, the funds cannot be repatriated through the three common mechanisms discussed in Chapter 11:

- **Dividends**
- **Intercompany fees**
- **Intercompany loans and loan repayments**

Foreign third-party payments of fees and prices owed directly to the multinational parent, as opposed to a foreign subsidiary, may also be prohibited.

All of these payments can be restricted by being declared either temporarily or permanently illegal. More often, they must require merely the approval of the local government or central bank. Such approval will usually depend on the foreign exchange available to the government and its own priorities regarding imports and exports related to the payments.

These problems must all be treated as unique and handled on a case-by-case basis. Yet, the following categories have helped to direct multinational corporate treasurers to appropriate solutions:[1]

- **Blocked funds**—Cannot be used at all by the parent or any affiliate.
- **Severely restricted**—Can be used *only* locally.
- **Restricted funds**—Can be used *only* to purchase parent's country's currency for remittance at a discount or through open market transactions, such as sales to brokers.

TYPES OF FUNDS

There are basically two types of funds involved:

- **Cash equivalents**—For example:
  —Cash at banks
  —Securities
- **Receivables**—Owed to the parent company and not paid only for the lack of foreign exchange/remittance approval.

Obviously, the different forms of the funds may have an impact on a corporation's ability to use a given type of remedy to solve the blocked funds problems. For example, you cannot sell local currency for dollars if you do not have the funds but are merely waiting to receive payment owed by a third party in the foreign country. Yet, a cooperative third party can often arrange to make any payments to the multinational corporation's local account or to a local buyer of the currency. Of course, the key word is "cooperative," and only some third parties are truly desirous of helping others to collect money from them.

GOVERNMENT APPROVAL FOR NORMAL REMITTANCE CHANNELS

Perhaps the easiest method of unblocking funds is to obtain the right for remittance of dividends, intercompany fees, intercompany loan payments, and third-party payments to the corporation. Even if these are prevented in the manner to which we are accustomed in the United States, approval by the appropriate government agency or the central bank can still be obtained in many cases after enough pressure is exerted, so that the payments are ultimately allowed. A well-presented request to the appropriate authorities by one of the following parties may make the difference:

- **Local management**
- **Local counsel**
- **Local bank**
- **Local consultant/lobbyist**

Also, careful documentation of the transaction may be all that is required to obtain approval. A properly worded invoice or loan document may allow intercompany obligations to be paid as an arm's-length obligation—merely upon review by one or more of the appropriate authorities and parties cited above.

STRATEGIES TO USE BLOCKED FUNDS

Once the normal channels are abandoned or at least appear less likely to be allowed, special strategies to use or remit blocked and restricted funds should be fully explored. This should be done in both a thorough and methodical manner.

Four strategies have traditionally been employed successfully for these purposes:

- **Delayed collection of receivables** from subsidiaries and third parties can prevent local placement of the funds where they can become permanently blocked. If merely a delay is required before normal remittance channels can be used—for administrative reasons or due to a shortage of foreign currency available to the government—documentation on the imports, dividends, and so on, should be preserved. Yet, once the funds are locally transferred to the multinational corporation, this documentation may become null and void; and there is no longer any legal rationale on which to remit the funds from the corporation's local bank account. At CBS, this has been a standard procedure in many countries for dividends and management fees from foreign subsidiaries and for royalties from licensees.
- **Maximum local use** possibilites should be sought for any funds, both cash and receivables. Some examples that are regularly employed are travel expenses for multinational corporate personnel visiting the country on business and the holding of management conferences in the affiliate within the corporation for some other business. At CBS, the local news and sports coverage bureaus have often been funded by blocked funds from other parts of the company.
- **Countertrade and barter** can be used to remit proceeds from blocked funds in the form of other goods. Yet, this is rarely a practical opportunity for many companies, which are not involved in the importing or marketing of the types of goods that can be brought home. While more fungible goods, such as cars, with broad markets and relatively fixed market prices, could be used by more companies, such goods may not be as readily available for countertrade or barter by local governments. (For example, CBS failed to obtain Yugo automobiles from Yugoslavia.) Finally, if the countertrade is not lined up with government approval before the transaction that generates the blocked funds is begun, the local government may be more reluctant to

make goods available, since some incremental exports might then be lost.

- **Discount sales of currency or cash equivalents,** in return for hard currency paid to the multinational corporation's bank account in another country, can solve the blocked funds problem—but at a cost of the discount percentage. You must also check the legality carefully on the front end. Brokers and banks may make or arrange the purchase. The ultimate user of the blocked funds may be a local resident or another multinational corporation that needs currency to operate in the country. This type of strategy has been used successfully in several countries around the world. However, the discounts can vary from 10 percent to 70 percent.

One nontraditional strategy, parallel loans, has often been touted as a means of repatriating blocked funds. However, we have never seen this used successfully in the true sense of repatriation.[2] For example, three separate banks and one multinational corporation proposed to solve CBS's $3-4 million problem with blocked Greek drachmas before Greece joined the EEC. CBS in Greece would have loaned drachmas to another corporation or deposited them in a given bank. The affiliate of the corporation or bank in the United States would then have loaned money to CBS in the United States.

We were told that this was really an intercompany loan mechanism implemented through third parties to make it legal. The problem is that unlike intercompany loans, the parallel loans are not eliminated upon consolidation of the financial loan payable and receivable in the United States. Both would remain on the corporate books. Thus, total capital and excess funds could not be reduced, which is the primary purpose of repatriation, as outlined in Chapter 11. However, under U.S. generally accepted accounting principles, there is one exception: if the parallel loans claim a right of setoff, when default on either loan in either country allows nonpayment of the other loan in the other country. Yet, for most countries in which funds are blocked, linkage of the two parallel loans with a right of setoff would be illegal. This is the reason that CBS never used parallel loans in Greece.

In practice, there is another exception or a reason to use parallel loans. If the rate earned by the corporation in the blocked funds country and the rate paid in the multinational parent's country are higher or lower than market value, respectively, this may be a desirable use of excess funds. Yet, the funds must still be considered blocked, even if some benefit results.

CLASSIFICATION MONITORING MECHANISM

For firms with blocked or restricted funds in several currencies, a routine system can monitor the various situations. The type of report used at CBS is shown in Table 14-1.

TABLE 14-1: *BLOCKED FUNDS STATUS REPORT*

Country	*Subsid. Division*	*Type of Funds*	*Classification*	*Amount LCY*	*$ Equiv.*	*Status/ Strategy*
Transylvania	Broadcast	Certificates of deposit	Severely restricted	1,000	100	Use for news bureaus
Valhalla	Records	Receivables	Restricted	5,000	200	Obtain local payment for sale at 20% discount

The report helps keep in focus the very different types of circumstances involved and the very different types of strategies required to solve the problems. Blocked funds are not one problem, but a general category of problems and circumstances, each of which needs to be addressed quite specifically.

SUMMARY AND CONCLUSIONS

International business involves the generation of proceeds due to the multinational corporation or cash equivalents owned by the corporation in different currencies in different countries. In the United States, these funds can usually be paid or transferred at will to other countries, provided that the underlying business transactions do not violate any laws. However, in other countries the funds can become blocked or restricted by the local governments, even if there is no taint whatsoever of illegality.

The funds can be classified according to the magnitude of the restrictions placed on them:

- **Blocked**—No use by the corporation allowed
- **Severely Restricted**—Only local use allowed
- **Restricted**—Can still be sold on open market for other currencies

The funds can also be classified according to their type or form:

- **Cash Equivalents**—Held by the corporation
- **Receivables**—Owed to the corporation

When funds first become blocked or restricted, every effort should be made to obtain government approval for some normal type of remittance through normal channels by:

- **Local management**
- **Local counsel**
- **Local bank**
- **Local consultant/lobbyist**

Reviewing the documentation with local authorities to show that the underlying transaction and proposed payment are in compliance with local laws is obviously most helpful for this purpose.

However, when normal channels fail, the following four strategies are used most often to solve a blocked funds problem:

- **Delayed collection of receivables**—To avoid becoming permanently blocked.

- **Maximum local usage**—By all parts of the corporation where possible.
- **Countertrade barter**—To take goods in kind as proceeds versus cash.
- **Discount sales to third parties**--To get less cash, but in hard currency in another, unblocked country.

A less traditional solution is a pair of parallel loans between the multinational corporation affiliates in the blocked country and another country and a third party operating in both countries. However, we have never seen this work satisfactorily to repatriate blocked funds by reducing excess cash and capital for the overall corporation.

To maximize the effectiveness of repatriating blocked funds, a routine program and summary status report should be maintained, ideally in chart form. This allows the corporate treasury staff to focus quickly and continuously on the special circumstances and strategies that are relevant for each of the quite different sets of circumstances involved and to react quickly whenever opportunities to repatriate or use the funds temporarily arise.

FOOTNOTES

1. Krackov, "International Cash Management for a Multinational Corporation," working paper, Institute of International Banking, Pace University, 1987, p. 18.
2. Ibid. pp. 18-19.

SELECTED REFERENCES

Adullah, Fuad A., *Financial Management for the Multinational Firm*, Prentice-Hall, 1987, Chapter 8.

Eiteman, David K. and Arthur I. Stonehill, with a contribution by Donald R. Lessard, *Multinational Business Finance*, Addison-Wesley, Fourth Edition, 1986, Chapter 15.

Krackov, Lawrence M., "International Cash Management for a Multinational Corporation," *Working Papers,* Institute of International Banking, Pace University, 1987.

Shapiro, Alan C., *Multinational Financial Management,* Allyn and Bacon, Second Edition, 1986, Chapter 10.

Index